THE LITTLE BOOK OF Restorative Justice for *People in Prison*

Rebuilding the Web of Relationships

BARB TOEWS

Intercourse, PA 17534
800/762-7171
www.GoodBooks.com

Credits

The diagram on page 61 is based loosely on a model by Paul McCold and Ted Wachtel of the International Institute for Restorative Practices. See P. McCold, "Toward a Mid-Range Theory of Restorative Criminal Justice: A Reply to the Maximalist Model," *Contemporary Justice Review* 3 (2000), 257-414. (The diagram is on page 401.) Used by permission.

Cover photograph by Howard Zehr.

Design by Dawn J. Ranck

THE LITTLE BOOK OF RESTORATIVE JUSTICE FOR PEOPLE IN PRISON

International Standard Book Number: 978-1-56148-523-9

Library of Congress Catalog Card Number: 2006016545

Library of Congress Cataloging-in-Publication Data

Toews, Barb.

The little book of restorative justice for people in prison : rebuilding the web of relationships / Barb Toews.

p. cm.

Includes bibliographical references.

ISBN-13: 978-1-56148-523-9 (pbk.)

1. Restorative justice. 2. Criminals--Rehabilitation. 3. Victims of crimes--Rehabilitation. 4. Prison psychology. I. Title.

HV8688.T64 2006

365'.66--dc22

2006016545

Table of Contents

Acknowledgments

This *Little Book* grows out of my work with men and women incarcerated in Pennsylvania prisons, especially those in Dallas, Graterford, Huntingdon, Muncy, Retreat, Rockview, and Smithfield. These people have been both supportive and critical of restorative justice. They have also granted me great patience as I learned from them and grew in my own understanding of this approach.

This book would not be possible without those who reviewed different versions of this manuscript. I thank all those who participated in manuscript focus groups in Pennsylvania: Preston Pfeifly, Derek Smith, Jon Yount, Tony Brown, Tommy Casillas, Steven Sanabria, Kevin Taylor, Judith Pomoroy, Eunika Simms, Linda Crisman, Charmaine Pfender, Sharon Wiggins, Marie Scott, Tonya Krout, Wendy Chiari, John Prichard, Dave Craig, Albert Bandy, Alonzo Watts, Paul Perry, and Wayne Covington. I apologize if I have inadvertently missed anyone!

I also thank those who participated in manuscript focus groups at Oregon State Prison: Robert Dietrich, Sam Sophanthavong, Tommie D. Maxwell, Antonio S. Palacios, Kevin Finckel, Roland Gray, Melissa Crabbe, Karuna Thompson, David Benedicktus, Fred Perloff, William Wood, and others who wish to remain anonymous.

Thanks go to Danny Malec, Kirsten Rothrock, and Tamara Mihalic, who facilitated these focus groups and reviewed draft manuscripts. I also offer my appreciation to the men and women who participated in preliminary focus groups at Graterford and Muncy, prior to the start of writing.

I especially thank Tanya Krout, Marie Scott, Alonzo Watts, Paul Perry, Preston Pfeifly, Kevin Canady, Michael Moore, and Russell Selby, who offered welcomed feedback on one of the final drafts. And a special thanks to Steven Palmer, incarcerated at Bellamy Creek Correctional Facility in Indiana.

I thank the Pennsylvania Prison Society, my bosses, and co-workers who share my commitment and compassion for people in prison. In particular, I thank Bill DiMascio, Betty-Ann Izenman, Naima Black, Ted Enoch, and Ann Schwartzman.

I also thank all those who read the manuscript and challenged me along the way, especially Danny Malec; Angela Trop; Kathy Buckley of the Office of the Victim Advocate; Joanne Torma, Deputy Superintendent of State Correctional Institution at Muncy; and Jen Alexander.

I also thank other restorative-justice practitioners from whose writings and work I have learned, even though I haven't met many of them. In particular, I thank Howard Zehr for encouraging my efforts to expand restorative justice to better represent the perspectives of those who have offended, and for inviting me to write this book.

And, since writing a *Little Book* is no little task, I give great thanks to my husband, Rod, for supporting and tolerating me and the project for the past two years.

1. Introduction

A woman from another block talks about you behind your back. Everything she says is a lie. You've tried to ignore her but she just keeps it up. What should happen next?

Your paroled loved one steals several hundred dollars from a safe at work. He spends the money getting high. He lies when confronted by his boss. What should happen next?

You receive word that someone murdered your sibling. Several months later, you discover that this person is incarcerated in your prison. What should happen next?

These dilemmas raise questions about justice. But *what is justice?*

Some people say that justice requires a good old-fashioned beating, revenge, punishment, or prison. The criminal-justice system often responds in the same way. This system believes that people who offend deserve to be punished for their crimes. Unfortunately, the resulting punishment may cause further harm to the offender, victim, offender's family, and the community.

Restorative justice answers the justice question in a different way. Restorative justice argues that crime destroys people and relationships. Justice, then, must repair and rebuild people and relationships. Incarcerated men and women have defined restorative justice in the following ways:

- It heals broken relationships and abuses, by people and for people.
- It builds instead of blames.
- It confronts a situation and helps those involved find a place of understanding, healing, and acceptance of each other.
- It works to make life better for others and for oneself.

Some say that restorative justice is what their grandmothers taught them: Respect yourself and others, clean up your messes, and treat others as you want to be treated.

A restorative-justice approach differs from the traditional criminal-justice approach. For sure, both strive for *accountability*. But the two approaches understand accountability differently.

Restorative justice understands accountability as addressing needs and making right the wrongs. Rather than focusing primarily on punishment for the offender, accountability focuses on the needs of victims as well as the needs and obligations of offenders, offender families, and communities.

> To do justice, people and relationships must be repaired.

The restorative philosophy starts with victims—the harms they experienced and their needs for repair. Helping an offender become accountable is a step toward restoring the victim. Offenders recognizing their obligation to their victims is the foundation of restorative justice.

In addition to accountability, restorative justice also offers a response to the complex experiences and needs of those who offend. People who have committed a crime, particularly those in prison, are also concerned with:

- their own personal experiences with victimization;
- healing from both offending and victimization;

- involvement in determining and meeting their own needs;
- their families;
- prevention of crime and reduction in recidivism;
- social justice, individual power, and the ability to have influence at the societal level;
- ways to practice restorative justice in daily life, without formal programs.

Restorative justice addresses many of these issues. This *Little Book* invites discussion about all of these areas of concern. For nonincarcerated readers, I hope this book increases your understanding of restorative justice for offenders.

About this *Little Book*

This *Little Book* grows out my restorative-justice work at the Pennsylvania Prison Society, a nonprofit agency serving and advocating for people in prison and their families.[1] The book represents years of dialogue with incarcerated men and women, often in restorative-justice seminars. As we talked and listened, the seminar curriculum evolved to include prisoners' perspectives and interests. This book is designed to approach restorative justice in much the same way as the Prison Society seminars.

The goals of this *Little Book* are twofold. First, this book aims to provide the reader with a working knowledge of restorative justice. Second, for those who embrace the philosophy, it suggests restorative practices or applications that are useful in prison and in daily life.

The book is organized to meet these two goals. Chapters 2 through 4 introduce the restorative-justice philosophy. Chapters 5 through 9 outline the justice needs of the community, victims, offenders, and offender families. Chapter

10 presents common restorative practices. Chapters 11 and 12 explore if and how these practices can be used in prison, and they present restorative justice as a way of life, including practical suggestions for use while incarcerated.

This book draws on the insights and understandings of incarcerated men and women who have been my teachers and broadened my understanding of restorative justice. I've learned that the philosophy speaks to them in meaningful and hopeful ways.

As one individual told me, "restorative justice connects with what is in our hearts" about responsibility and making amends. Another talked about "the human drive to want to make things right and to build peace." Still another sees restorative justice as part of the journey for "a greater good and for personal growth." These individuals have actively sought ways to make amends to their victims.

It's important for me to say a word about the perspective from which this book is written. I have never been a victim of crime or a criminal offender, and as such, I can only speak from this perspective. However, as a restorative-justice practitioner working with people in prison, I am trained and committed to balancing the needs of both offenders and victims.

Many of the prisoner perspectives that shaped this book come from African Americans who lived in inner-city Philadelphia and who received life sentences for violent crimes. Many were young, poor, and undereducated prior to incarceration. Consequently, I write from a framework primarily of those who have experienced violent, urban street crime. This framework cannot and does not speak for everyone.

Each individual experience as an "offender" or "prisoner" is unique. Experiences vary depending on whether, for instance, one is poor or wealthy, white or a person of color, ur-

One night in 1974, two young men vandalized 22 homes, cars, and businesses. At the request of the probation officer and his colleague, the judge ordered the men to meet with their victims. The men began to knock on the victims' doors, stating who they were and asking what they owed for the damages. One victim was ready to punch the men. Another invited them in for tea. Within three months the men paid back all their victims. These men participated in the first documented face-to-face victim-offender meetings ordered by a court.

Decades later, one of these men, Russ, was studying law and security at a local college. A guest speaker from a community-justice center talked about a local celebrated case that inspired a restorative-justice movement. Russ realized they were talking about him! He had no idea his experience as an offender had become an example of a different way to do justice. Russ later became a volunteer mediator with the program.[2]

ban or rural, young or old, or highly educated or undereducated. There are many additional factors that give meaning to crime, its causes and prevention, and ideas about justice. Therefore, it is impossible to speak to the specific and unique life stories of all who may read this book.

At times, I use labels like "prisoner," "offender," and "victim." I want to acknowledge, though, that these labels have the potential to dehumanize and lock people into one single identity. As humans, we have the potential to both hurt and to be hurt, to be both victim and offender. So these labels have pitfalls. Still, when they are used to identify only part of a person or a particular act, they do have some value. They provide a way to identify those with a "stake" in a situation of wrongdoing, for example. Moreover, to admit that one is an "offender" is a step toward accountability. So I use these labels, aware of their limitations and dangers.

How to use this *Little Book*

This *Little Book* is a sampler or "teaser." It will likely raise as many questions as it answers. I hope these questions, discussions, and criticisms create the chance to learn more about restorative justice.

The case studies at the beginning of each chapter offer practical examples of restorative justice at work. Some stories tell of common restorative practices. Others reflect unique ways of applying restorative values. A few even express the challenges of doing restorative justice. All are intended to spark ideas about how you can be part of restorative justice yourself.

The chapters will further fuel thought and discussion on a variety of topics that range from personal to academic. You may find the following questions useful in your reflection:

1. What does the chapter mean to you in light of your personal experiences?
2. In what ways have you seen or experienced the concepts in real life?
3. With what do you agree? Why?
4. With what do you disagree? Why?
5. What benefits and risks are there to applying restorative justice in prison?
6. What would it take to apply the concepts in your life?

The final two chapters include suggestions for practicing justice in prison and in daily life. Many of these suggestions come from men and women who are in prison. These are meant to jump-start your own ideas and help you consider how to practice restorative justice in any context or setting.

There are many ways to use this *Little Book.* You may read it on your own or lead a discussion group using the book as a text. You can use the book in an existing prison program, possibly reading it with family or prison staff.

This book may raise difficult issues for you. Perhaps you are a crime victim, struggle with family relationships, or deal with feelings of guilt and shame. I hope you'll find healing ways to explore your emotions. Some have used art, journaling, or talking to a friend as way of getting things out.

My hope is that this *Little Book* will start—or continue—your own journey of discussion, accountability, and healing on the restorative-justice path.

2. Web of Relationships

Late one January evening, Tony, a teenager, shot and killed Tariq Khamisa, a young pizza-delivery man. In the face of profound grief, Azim Khamisa, Tariq's father, wanted to do something good in Tariq's name. He reached out to Ples Felix, Tony's grandfather. Together they created an agency committed to violence prevention among youth. Through this experience, Mr. Felix "realized we had the potential to not only help heal each other, but perhaps contribute to the healing of people we didn't even know."[3]

Khamisa's and Felix's experiences imply that everyone is connected. Both pain and healing are shared. Restorative justice grows out of these shared connections. Before exploring the philosophy in more detail, this chapter introduces the importance of strong connections and the implications of broken connections between people.

Connection

Imagine you sit in a circle of chairs. One by one, people whom you are close to sit down with you. Then others who have touched your life but with whom you are not as close join you. People continue to join the circle: family, friends, co-workers, prison staff, and members of your faith community.

Included in the circle are elements of nature such as plants, animals, air, and water. Soon the chairs are full with all the people and elements that have touched your life, past and present. Now connect each of these individuals and elements with a single, crisscrossing strand of string to form a web.

Human life grows out of this web of relationships. Through strong connections to others, we meet our basic needs for safety, love, self-worth, comfort, and even food and shelter. In a strong web, *everyone is equal* in worth, access to power, and the right to a meaningful life. No one person is more valuable than another. There is no "us" or "them."

Yet, *each individual is unique.* Relationships create stories which, in turn, create our individual identity. Family and friends, cultural and faith teachings, and even political and economic policies teach us who we are, how to act, and who we can become. Because our respective *relationships impact us as individuals,* the web becomes the "big picture" of who each of us are. To understand an individual is to understand his or her relationships.

On the other hand, *individuals impact relationships.* When one person is happy, the joy is shared across the web. When one treats another with respect, all experience respect.

The same holds true for pain. When one person hurts another, that action breaks the connection. When this happens, the spirit of the web calls people to repair the relationship. The web constantly moves and shifts as individuals build and repair relationships.

A strong web of relationships gives meaning and purpose to our lives. We are able to live to our fullest potential because we get and give what we need to live.

Disconnection

Relationships shape and support us, but they can also cause pain. Family, friends, and others let us down, put us down, abuse us, and ignore us. We do the same to them, intentionally and unintentionally. When left unattended, these broken relationships distort the web, forcing it out of balance.

Both interpersonal and societal *relationships can become unequal.* Some people win their happiness at the expense of others. Some people are considered good and others only bad. Some are deemed more worthy. Those who are deemed undeserving are usually shoved aside.

One doesn't have to look far for real-life examples. White people tend to have more power than people of color. Men may be valued more than women. The rich have more political clout than the poor. The free are seen as more worthy than the imprisoned. These inequalities play themselves out in the workplace, home, schools, government, and elsewhere.

Individuals lose part of themselves in these unjust webs. Broken relationships make it difficult to achieve one's life purpose. Accountability to each other is devalued. Individuals stand alone, sometimes engaged in a struggle against the world. When one person feels this way, the feeling travels across the web.

The image of the web helps us to understand how imbalances in our lives affect other people, and vice versa. It also provides a vision of how we might live together in an ideal community. Restorative justice aims at strengthening the web of community, and, in doing so, aims to meet individual needs.

3. Crime and Criminal Justice

Members of a community heard that a transition house for sex offenders was opening in their neighborhood. Expecting opposition, a concerned citizen suggested holding a Talking Circle. After careful preparation, about 70 community members and house residents attended. After listening to an opening children's story, Circle members talked about times when they were hurt by others, did something wrong, or felt unworthy.

Their conversation then turned to their concerns about having the home in the neighborhood. A few community members talked about personal experiences with sexual abuse. Without excusing their crimes, several of the offenders spoke to similar experiences. The Circle decided to accept the home and created a plan that worked for everyone. They worked together to get the house ready. All new house residents were introduced around the neighborhood. Several months later, when the city decided to move the house elsewhere, the community fought to keep it.[4]

Broken and unequal webs offer one way to understand crime and criminal justice. Individual nature is another influence of crime. This chapter explores disconnection among people and its impacts on crime and criminal justice.

Disconnection and crime

There are as many causes of crime as there are people. Yet, *crime is a sign that something is wrong with our relationships.* Crime occurs in a distorted world.

I have heard incarcerated men and women talk about crime by saying, "It was a high point in my life," or "People looked up to me," or "I had to prove that you couldn't mess with me." To me, these statements reflect a quest for respect, power, and self-worth. Many who made these comments saw few "legitimate," mainstream options to meet these needs. They chose crime. The statements do not excuse the crime. Rather, they offer a way to understand the individual's choice to offend.

Crime can be seen as an attempt to get justice for oneself.

Those who commit white-collar and corporate crime may also be searching for respect, power, and worth. People who commit these crimes have more access to mainstream sources of power and worth. But they hoard existing power or crave more power and wealth. Crime can be a way to protect what one has and get more of it, albeit at the expense of others.

Both types of crime come from broken webs. One group tries to get what is missing and denied them. The other group tries to keep what they have or to get more of it. Both crimes can be seen as an attempt to get justice for oneself.[5] Both can be seen as an attempt to get what one "deserves."

This justice, however, is a false one. It doesn't build relationships as justice should. Rather, the offending individual further destroys the web. Pain is exchanged for pain. Those who experience the crime—victims, offender family members, or others in the community—feel violated and disrespected. They are fearful and feel powerless over their lives. They come to view themselves and the world differently. They and their relationships change. Some people deal with this pain by offending against others. Others search for other ways to respond to this added pain.

An unjust response to an unjust world leads to unjust communities. I listen as incarcerated men and women talk about the daily life of street "wars" and the resulting "casualties" and "post-traumatic street syndromes." I watch as dedicated workers lose retirement money due to corporate greed and power. Both are "cultures of crime" that create more disconnection.

Disconnection and criminal justice

Often the criminal-justice system has much the same effect as crime itself. It further breaks the web rather than repairs it. The system is basically organized to answer three questions:[6]

1. What law was broken?
2. Who did it?
3. What do they deserve?

These questions focus on ensuring that the offender gets what he or she "deserves." The system shows little respect for people who offend. They are typically seen as wholly bad and unworthy people who deserve little more than blame, pain, and punishment.

With more than two million people in jails and prisons in the United States, punishment is frequently incarceration. There are few opportunities for meaningful accountability, especially to victims, or for personal healing or growth. This justice approach adds more disconnection and brokenness.

In some ways, criminal justice can reflect the same values of the crime itself: an attempt to make sure people get what they "deserve," to receive their "just-deserts."

The offender focus of the justice system ignores the many people impacted by a crime—victims, offenders' families, and communities. Victims experience exclusion from the justice process. The state replaces the victim. This is evident with the language of "The State vs. Joe/Jane Offender."

Since the crime is officially against the state, victims have few chances to talk about the crime and what justice means to them. The system wipes its hands of victims when the offender is sentenced, and sometimes before. In doing so, the justice process denies victims their humanity as people hurt by the crime.

Criminal justice often disrespects people and their needs.

Offenders' families also experience the impact of a crime. Yet they, too, are excluded from the justice process. The system gives them little opportunity to assist and support their loved one, let alone respond to their familial needs. They have few avenues for holding their loved ones accountable. For those families who feel obligated to the crime victims, there are few formal avenues to make amends on their loved one's behalf. Since they are seen as irrelevant to the justice process, families remain cut off from justice, from their loved ones, and from the community.

The justice process also pushes aside the community. The community feels the crime in individual and relational ways. It also has a vested interest in both the offender and victim. Yet, the justice process doesn't invite the community to talk about a crime's impact or to support victims and offenders. Nor does the system challenge the community to explore the causes of crime. Because community members have only minimal information about the justice participants, they develop simplistic stereotypes of victims, offenders, and offenders' families. Since community members are merely observers to the justice process, community remains broken.

The criminal-justice process disrespects offenders, victims, offender families, and community by denying the human experience of crime. It's part of the distorted web. It ignores the "big picture" that makes up people's lives.

Criminal justice can be seen as a power struggle with clear winners and losers. Some people have more power (for instance, judges and the wealthy) while others have less or none at all (for instance, victims, offenders, and the poor). Those with power make decisions on behalf of those without power.

The criminal-justice system usually results in simplistic, "one-size-fits-all" sentences. These sentences do little to promote change and healing. Individuals, relationships, and community remain broken. True justice, on the other hand, requires that people participate in ways that respect their experiences and relationships, and strives to transform them.

4. Restorative Justice

Sitting quietly with rapt attention, 1,400 incarcerated men and women witnessed the intense emotions of more than 20 victims of violent crime. They were watching, with community members, the play, A Body in Motion. *Debriefing sessions gave audience members a chance to explore their reactions. Some expressed remorse for their crimes. Others told of their own victimization—for instance, a murdered child or an abusive parent. All expressed a desire to carry the message of healing and accountability to others.*

It all started when a group of incarcerated men requested a single performance. Through a unique collaboration between prisoners, offender and victim-service providers, prison administrators, faith communities, and a committed funder, the prisoners' request became a tour with performances in eight prisons and seven communities. This diverse group of partners discovered common ground. The tour humanized victims while honoring the experiences of offenders and communities.[7]

Restorative justice rebuilds the web of relationships by putting *people* back into the justice process. This type of justice promotes change and healing among individuals, relationships, and society as a whole.

I define restorative justice this way:

Restorative justice is a way to do justice that actively includes the people impacted by crime—victims, offenders, their families, and communities. Its goal is to respect and restore each as individuals, repair broken relationships, and contribute to the common good.

Restorative questions and assumptions

Restorative justice is a *"needs-based"* understanding of justice. It asks very different questions than the "deserts-based" criminal-justice system. Restorative justice asks:

1. Who has been hurt?
2. What does he or she need?
3. Who should be involved in meeting those needs?
4. What is the best way to repair the harm and meet those needs?

The questions are first asked of victims. But they are also asked of the other justice participants—offenders, their families, and communities. No one can answer on anyone's behalf. And these questions apply to both the *causes* and *impacts* of crime.

These questions carry *restorative beliefs* such as:

- Every person counts.
- Everyone needs to be respected, heard, and understood.
- Everyone deserves to be treated justly.
- Everyone is capable of change and healing if his or her needs are met.
- Justice requires accountability that changes and heals people and relationships.
- People create justice together.

Justice is no longer one swift, single, punitive sentence. Restorative justice requires thoughtful reflection and deliberation in order to fully understand the crime and individual needs. This type of justice takes hard work but leads to meaningful accountability and long-term healing.

Key restorative-justice elements

The focus on *harm* and *accountability* ground restorative justice in the web. Restorative justice discovers how victims and communities have been harmed by a crime, and how the offender and his or her family have been impacted. Once harms and impacts are known, the philosophy explores what people need to deal with a crime. This exploration includes addressing an offender's accountability for the crime and his or her need to make amends.

> Restorative justice is a path to personal and societal healing.

Restorative justice actively involves each justice participant in "doing justice." Victims have an active say in the justice process and in deciding what they need. Offenders are no longer justice "recipients." They are actors who strive to understand the crime and determine how to be accountable. Their families and the broader community play a role. *Participation* makes it possible to successfully meet each participant's unique needs.

As we will see later, some forms of restorative justice allow offenders and victims to meet or communicate with each other. However, participation in restorative justice does not require victims and offenders to come in contact with each other. And the participation of one does not deny the participation of another. The justice process expands to include and accommodate everyone.

In a restorative approach, justice seeks to *restore* and *heal* the justice participants. Rather than focusing on pain for pain, restorative justice strives to rebuild people and relationships. Justice is about "making things right." This journey toward healing is guided by a commitment to "do no harm" to the justice participants. As a result, justice rebuilds the web of relationships rather than further weakens it.

Restorative values

Restorative justice is grounded in values that affirm and build a strong web. Four core values are *respect, care, trust,* and *humility.*

A justice system grounded in *respect* recognizes the need for accountability, restoration, and healing. This respect comes through listening to and validating the experiences of everyone impacted by crime. Because it is designed to treat everyone with dignity and worth, a respectful system assists people in naming their justice needs and involves them in creating the justice response.

A restorative-justice process acts with *care* when it values both individual accountability and mutual responsibility. In doing so, the system sees the shared humanity in everyone impacted by a crime. Such a system strives to "do no harm" and wants the best for everyone. A caring system believes that people can grow and heal if their needs are met, and acts to make that healing possible.

A *trustworthy* justice system promotes the common good as it advocates for accountability and healing. Justice operates with openness and honesty. It values consistency, dependability, and confidentiality. Justice processes are designed to balance and share power with the justice participants as they create the justice response.

Participation requires justice *humility*. A humble justice system does not assume that it knows everything and has all the answers. Rather, it strives to learn from and understand everyone affected by crime. The system accepts that the individuals impacted by crime know their experiences and needs best. Further, humble justice processes make it possible for people to participate, collaborate, and cooperate. And, because each individual is different, the system embraces and creates space for the inevitable questions, uncertainties, and complexities.

Restorative Values –

- Respect
- Care
- Trust
- Humility

It may be difficult to imagine that a fully restorative justice system *is* possible or that all parties impacted by crime would be willing to participate in a restorative process. Yet the philosophy and its current practices hold promise to transform people impacted by crime and the criminal-justice system itself. Case studies throughout the book show real ways that people have used restorative justice in small ways to have big impact.

Restorative justice offers a justice response that seeks to restore individuals, repair relationships, and promote the common good. By looking at both the harms and causes of crime, the philosophy promotes a justice that "makes things right" for victims, offenders, their families, and communities. The next chapters explore needs and "making things right" through the eyes of each justice participant. This look begins with community.

5. Reconnecting Community

Hollow Water, a First-Nations community in Northern Canada, was struggling. Substance abuse, suicide, and violence permeated the lives of their children. These problems grew out of community-wide and intergenerational sexual abuse, family violence, and substance abuse. In turn, these experiences stemmed from the physical violence and cultural destruction caused by the first white settlers.

Residents of Hollow Water watched for many years as abuse victims among them suffered in silence. Offenders went off to jail and returned with little change. As a community, they decided to "do justice" themselves. Through participatory, community-created programs, offenders were expected to accept responsibility for their actions, not deny it. Victims were encouraged to talk of their experiences, not keep silent. Lost traditions and teachings were embraced, not degraded. The community turned itself around, becoming a community in which everyone got on the "healing path."[8]

Individual healing affects community health. Some think that the "restorative" in restorative justice means that people go back to the way things were before a crime. The Hollow Water experience suggests that "restorative" means healing both community and its individual members so all can move *forward* with their lives. Restorative justice points the way toward a strong community that can create strong individuals. For this reason, we look at community justice needs before individual needs.

But what is "community?" Generally, there are two types: communities of care and broader communities. *Communities of care* include people we care about, and who care about us, on a personal level. These communities generally consist of family and friends. *Broader communities* include those relationships that are less personal and are based on geography or membership. For instance, these communities may include neighborhoods, cities, social or work clubs, or faith and ethnic groups.

Restorative justice is more about going forward than going back.

Crime impacts both types of communities, and both communities can help to cause a crime. Yet, the criminal-justice system provides few opportunities for either kind of community to be involved in justice. If anything, the criminal-justice system ignores community so that it becomes a "bystander."

Without understanding the personal impact of a crime on both victims and offenders, community members may not see either victims or offenders as people in need of healing and accountability. Instead, community members often develop simplistic and negative stereotypes of victims and offenders, and thus miss the chance to support individuals, repair relationships, and heal as a community.

A community can be both "offender" and "victim." A community may, in some situations, need to repair harms caused. In other situations, it may need to receive for harms it experienced. Offender and victim communities of care are addressed in later chapters. This chapter focuses on the six justice needs of the broader community.

Community justice needs

Imagine a vibrant and healthy forest. Such a forest gives life to many different plants and animals. However, without the right amounts of air, water, and fire, one species dies while another's population explodes. One change in the natural balance alters the environment for all living beings. Restoring the ecosystem's health can take decades, if not centuries.

A community is a delicate ecosystem, like this forest. With the right mix of respect and equality, a healthy community gives life to all the people within it. Without balance, some people flourish while others barely make it. And just one event, such as a crime, can impact a community for years to come. (This ecosystem analogy is not to suggest that environment is the only factor that influences how people act. Humans have personalities and natures that shape how they act and respond to others.)

A community has its own set of justice needs essential to restoring the balance in the web of relationships. Even when not directly affected, community members feel and react to crime in much the same way as individual crime victims. People deadbolt their doors and windows when others are burglarized. They lock their car doors and windows to avoid theft. They become suspicious of, and fear, others. Community members grieve with those who have been assaulted or murdered. They worry about it happening to them or their loved ones. They see themselves in the face of others who are victims.

As a result, communities require *attention to their needs as a group impacted by crime*. These needs occur at two levels: individually and collectively. Those who are physically or emotionally close to a crime may need individual and personal attention. These people may be friends, neighbors, or co-workers of crime victims.

Collective responses serve groups of people who are further removed from, but yet affected by, the crime. For instance, those who deal drugs may appear, on the surface, to harm no one. Yet, the neighborhood and its residents experience personal fear and neighborhood decay. The crime's social and financial costs cannot be calculated. But there needs to be a collective justice response to deal with the impacts.

Because offending is a sign that something is wrong, a community is obligated to *be in relationship with those who offend and their loved ones.* In this relationship, offenders and their loved ones remain as valued community members and receive assistance in meeting their justice needs of healing and accountability to others. In doing so, the community and offender discover their mutual responsibility to each other.

A community also has an obligation to *be in relationship with victims and their loved ones.* Ignoring the victims adds to the original insult of the crime. This relationship recognizes victims as valued community members and respects them as individuals. Communities need to actively assist victims in meeting their individual needs for justice and healing. This relationship is also about mutual responsibility. For instance, community concern for victims draws victims in so that they are less likely to seek retaliation or revenge against the offender or someone else.

Being in relationship with offenders, victims, and their communities of care requires a *commitment to values such as respect, trust, care,* and *humility.* Without such values, a community risks crime happening again. This call to life-giving values challenges a community to look at how its members

A restorative community will:

- Attend to its needs as a group when it has been impacted by crime.
- Maintain relationships with those who offend and their loved ones.
- Maintain relationships with those who have been hurt and their loved ones.
- Commit to practicing values such as respect, care, trust, and humility.
- Work toward becoming a more equal and just society.
- Seek opportunities to participate in justice.

relate to each other. Moving from destructive to positive values is possible when a community sees the worth in each member and works for the good of all members.

These values create the opportunity for *change toward a more equal and just community.* A community can be dysfunctional in much the same way as a family can be. Restorative justice points toward social justice, a necessary element in crime prevention. So a community needs to explore how, through its structures, it offends against its members. For instance, do all members:

- feel respected and valued?
- feel like they belong in the community?
- act in the best interests of the whole community?
- have access to what they need to live?

"No" answers require changes in power imbalances, economic and educational disparity, racism, sexism, and other injustices. When those are addressed, large-scale social transformation can follow, to everyone's benefit.

In order to keep the six preceding practices, a community must *participate in the justice process.* It costs at least $20,000 to incarcerate one person for one year. Imagine if a community used that money to do justice, provide safety, and prevent future crime. Restorative justice believes that a community wants to promote the health of its individual members and the common good. However, to realize and act on these good intentions, a community has to be part of the process.

I find words like "hospitality" and "embrace" useful in imagining a community which acts restoratively. These words create images of welcome, togetherness, and a shared community life. Such images take us back to the idea of the web.

Some incarcerated individuals say that restorative justice is a way to build the experience of community which we want for our children and future generations. Building such a community creates a healthy environment that promotes a justice grounded in accountability and healing. Restorative justice requires cultivating a restorative community for the sake of its members.

6. Reconnecting Individuals

Dressed in black and red, a group of men and women gathered on stage. Some were mothers of murdered children. Others were parents of incarcerated children. Still others had been incarcerated themselves. Some had several of these identities. They were all performers in a play, Beyond the Walls, *created out of their own experiences. They did not act out another person's story; they expressed their own.*

A mother likens her neighborhood to a cemetery, the houses to tombstones. A man recounts his father's violent response to a lynching. Another mother reflects that she and the victim's family screamed the same scream. A sister now notices beauty around her because she knows that tomorrow it may be gone. The play brought these individuals together to give voice to their sorrow and pain and to the redemptive power of change. Together, they created a collective narrative.[10]

Restorative justice places the people impacted by crime at its center. Offenders, victims and their communities of care, and offender families are the key justice participants. All have their own unique justice needs. Meeting these needs promotes personal healing. And healed and healthy individuals, in turn, create strong communities.

Men and women in prison have been my greatest teachers on individual justice needs. Many of these individuals have experiences not only as an offender but also as a victim and as an offender family member. Having offended does not exclude someone from experiencing another crime as a victim. In spite of their differences, the needs of all these individuals have some important similarities.

The similar needs of offenders, offenders' families, and victims make sense. Individual justice needs emerge out of the web and reflect what people need for a meaningful life. This chapter introduces *eight individual justice needs.* The following three chapters explore these needs in more detail for victims, offenders, and offender families.

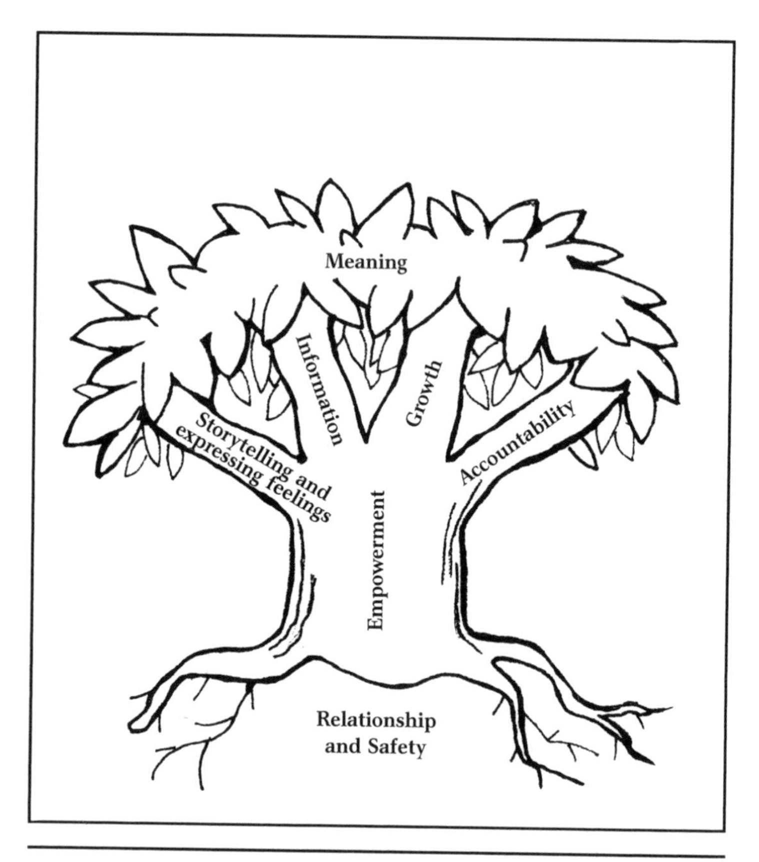

Individual justice needs

If community is a forest, individual community members are the trees. A strong and flourishing tree represents the eight individual justice needs. (See the diagram on p.32.)

The justice tree grows from its interconnected roots of *relationship* and *safety*. When faced with crime, its impacts and causes, people need to be grounded again (or for the first time) in safe relationships. Safe relationships are based on respect, care, trust, and humility and are free of judgment and shame. Safe relationships also include safety from physical harm.

The trunk represents *empowerment*. Like the backbone of a tree, empowerment is an individual's innate desire and ability to stand up, with strength and determination, to do the work of justice. Empowerment includes controlling one's life and participating in the actual justice process. With support from the roots, empowerment makes the work in the branches possible.

The branches symbolize the needs of *storytelling and venting feelings, information, growth,* and *accountability.* There is no particular order in meeting these needs.

Storytelling, or speaking from the heart about one's experience, and expressing feelings have a profound impact on people. The process helps them get things out and assists them in making sense of a crime's impacts and causes. When individuals can talk of their experiences, they receive needed respect, honor, and validation.[11]

Information promotes understanding as people seek answers to the practical and spiritual questions that follow crime. The need for personal and relational growth both requires and results from making sense of the crime.

Accountability, a fundamental restorative concept, relates directly to the impacts and causes of a specific crime.

It means "making things right" as much as one can. To do that, accountability requires: 1) an understanding of the unique harms of the crime and 2) statements of responsibility and actions to repair those harms, such as making amends and payment for losses. It is through accountability that victims and offenders can begin to let go of a crime's power.

> Restorative justice finds the right justice response for each person.

Meaning flourishes in the canopy of leaves and is the result of everything that has happened from the roots on up. With meaning, individuals incorporate the crime into their lives. They establish a new sense of self-identity based on what happened. They again understand their place in the world and in relationship to others. They experience renewed control and order to their lives. Wholeness emerges out of the brokenness. While the individual continues to grow and change like a tree, meaning symbolizes a place of justice.

Every tree has roots, a trunk, branches, and foliage. Yet, each tree is different. So it is with justice. While individuals often have similar needs, each person experiences crime differently, so meeting these needs will vary. Restorative justice seeks to understand these differences and find the right justice response for each person.

Trees are also dynamic and in constant movement as they change with the seasons. People experience crime and healing in much the same way. They change and move as they deal with the crime, even many years later. As a result, the word "closure" is inappropriate when talking about crime. Closure suggests that a crime and its aftermath end. But, the impact of a crime lives on, though in a different form. Even a tree remembers life in its rings. Other words like "recovery," "surviving," or "transcending" more accurately describe what happens after crime.

You may notice that forgiveness is not listed as a justice need. Forgiveness is very personal and it means different things to different people. I define it as when an individual lets go of the power that a crime has over him or her. One can forgive oneself or others. While the idea of forgiveness is comforting (especially the thought of receiving it), it is not easy to do. And, the forgiving person often does it for his or her own personal healing more than for that of another.

Those offenders, victims, and family members who choose forgiveness experience a deep sense of healing and movement toward meaning. Those who do not forgive may find other paths toward healing. Forgiveness remains a personal choice. Restorative justice respects each person's individual choice.

Trees need the roots, the leaves, and everything in between to flourish. Individuals need satisfaction of each of the eight justice needs to flourish. Safety and relationship make it possible to move toward meaning, and the work in the branches can contribute to safe relationships. Restorative justice makes it possible for people to move toward both relationship and meaning following a crime.

The next three chapters explore these eight justice needs from the perspectives of the victim, offender, and offender's family, in that order. However, you may read—or reread—these chapters in any order you prefer.

As you read, remember your personal life experiences. Perhaps, in addition to having committed a crime, you have been a robbery victim or have a child involved with the justice system. Your family may have experienced a crime as a victim. Or, perhaps you committed a crime against your family. Each chapter speaks to these complex and intertwined experiences.

7. Reconnecting Victims and Their Communities of Care

A drunk driver killed a young couple and their puppy. In memory of their loved ones, their families erected a memorial at the location of the crash. When the man responsible for the deaths became eligible for parole, the victims' families wanted him to do something meaningful in memory of the people he killed. The families' request was made available to the parole board. As part of his parole, the man was expected to work with his agent and the victim office to make a plan.

Through the parole officer, the families requested that the man regularly clean the memorial sight and repaint the crosses during the anniversary month of the crash. They also asked that he volunteer at the local animal shelter. The chance to make this request, and have it fulfilled, was powerful and meaningful for the families. They found a unique way to remember their children and work through their victimization. They began their healing journey on their own and took another step forward by holding accountable the man responsible in this way.[12]

Victims and their communities of care often experience crime as trauma. The crime disrupts the normal flow of life and throws things out of balance. Relationships are no longer the same. Safety and security seem fleeting. One's beliefs and values are called into question. Physical damages may radically alter one's ability to work and take care of family or even oneself. The unexpected financial costs tax family budgets. These are just a few ways in which people are impacted by crime.[13]

Crime victim Azim Khamisa describes the "emotional nuclear bomb" that landed when he learned of his son's murder.[14] This explosive image is apt for many victims regardless of the type of crime—nonviolent, violent, property, physical, white-collar, or street. The person whose car was stolen may feel some of the same feelings as someone whose child was murdered. The intensity may vary but the kinds of feelings are the same.

The effects of crime are long-lasting and far-reaching. The crime and its impacts can resurface days, months, and even years after the crime. Individuals may begin to feel the emotions associated with the crime as an anniversary date approaches. Marriages may end from the resulting stress years after the crime. An individual may lose the ability to fulfill his or her dreams. There is no linear path with an end on which to travel. Rather, the healing path is a winding one; some may pass the same spot more than once.

The reality that the criminal-justice system frequently ignores victims' experiences and needs does little to help victims deal with the crime and experience justice. While victims have only a small part, if any, in the criminal-justice process, they and their needs are central to restorative jus-

> *"You trust life not to injure you in this way . . . You trusted humanity not to have that ugly side to it . . . You have incredible expectations of others' behavior that just [don't] happen. Now I have no trust in others."*[15]

> *"It was like a twister coming through your house. You slowly have to clean up, fix the broken pieces, replace things. Eventually your home will become your home again."*[16]

tice. This chapter explores each of the eight justice needs in more detail from a victim's perspective.

Victim justice needs

Crime breaks relationships, and in doing so, contributes to feelings of insecurity. Restoring *safety* and *relationship* is key for victims. Many victims find their own way to physical safety. For instance, they replace locks, carry mace or guns, and install burglar bars and security systems. Yet, for some, no matter what they do, they never feel safe again. At times, they create their own prisons inside their homes, afraid to leave. Relationships are one way to provide physical safety.

Emotional safety is just as important. Restoring safety in this regard reestablishes one's faith and trust in others. Safe relationships are free of mistrust, manipulation, judgment, blame, and shame. Victims feel validated, believed, and heard in such relationships.

A person who offends has made a choice to commit the crime. Victims did not choose to be a victim; they had little, if any, control over the crime itself or its aftermath. As a result, every facet of a victim's life is unexpectedly disrupted. Victims often feel powerless. This reality makes *empowerment* particularly important. Victims need to regain control

> *"How do I get through the rest of my life? How do I live with the agony of having been cheated out of sharing my son's life."*[17]

of their lives. Personal control comes when victims are able to make decisions about how to deal with the crime and meet their needs. The chance to participate in the justice system is an important way to establish control.

The need for control is connected to the need for *information*. Most crimes leave questions in their wake. Victims may seek answers for practical questions such as: What happened? Why did it happen? Why me? Where are my belongings? How can I find out what is going on?

Other questions may be more introspective and personal: Why did I react the way I did? What is going on for me now? How do I go on? What is next for me?

Still others are spiritual in nature. Crime has the potential to challenge how one understands the world. When faced with a shaken worldview, one may question God and other higher powers as well as the meaning of life. Seeking answers is a way to regain control and move toward meaning.

Storytelling and venting feelings help victims get out what is inside, put the crime into perspective, and make sense of their reactions. Private ways to speak to one's experience and feelings include journaling; writing poetry; painting; or talking with family, friends, or therapists. Public means for storytelling and venting feelings often involve judicial or advocacy settings. For instance, a victim may choose to speak at a victims' rally, read an impact statement in court, or advocate for special legislation. When heard, victims experience much needed validation and affirmation.

Validation also grows out of *accountability*. Accountability has two features—restitution and vindication. When losses

> *"Not getting out [one's story] is like being constipated."*[18]

> *"When he said, 'You didn't put me [in prison]; I put myself here,' it was the most powerful thing he could have said, because he finally admitted it."*[19]

remain unpaid, a victim may experience financial devastation. Restitution is the offender's payment for the victim's financial losses. Vindication frees the victim from any responsibility for the crime. One way this occurs is when the offender accepts, or is assigned by the court, responsibility for the crime.

Financial restitution and vindication go hand in hand. When the offending person pays restitution, he or she makes a statement of responsibility. The payment carries the message, "I hurt you so these costs are mine to pay. You are not responsible." For some victims, the statement of responsibility means more than the money itself. As a result, even small restitution payments can take a victim one step further on his or her healing journey.

For victims, *growth* reflects the personal journey toward becoming a whole person. Even though victims did not choose the crime, the crime forces an opening for introspection and personal change. For some, this growth may be relational. For instance, one may deal with past experiences, set boundaries, or find new relationships. For others, this growth may be highly personal, resulting in insights about who they are, what they need, and areas of personal work. But when their needs are not met, victims may not grow, and may remain stuck in the hurt they have experienced.

> *"There is nothing like murder to make you really, really look at yourself, if you choose. It tears off scabs from things in the past."*[20]

> *"I don't want to just function; I want to heal. I want to transcend this."*[21]

The *meaning* victims find at the treetop is sometimes called a "new normal." Because life is different after a crime, what was normal before the crime is no longer normal. With a "new normal," victims take on a life and identity that include the crime. Like the rings in a tree, the crime remains part of their inner being and influences the future. Yet, they continue to thrive.

Victims experience crime in perhaps the most personal and direct ways. Restorative justice strives to create meaningful responses to the resulting needs. In doing so, victims experience reconnection to the web of relationships. In turn, the web itself becomes stronger.

8. Reconnecting Offenders

A group of men with long-term sentences recognized that their past behaviors, including their crimes, caused a lot of pain to their families, victims, and the community as a whole. They also realized that they shared a responsibility to these three groups that incarceration had not cancelled. In an attempt to repay this debt, the men organized a day-long program for men who would be soon going home and community guests.

The incarcerated organizers took turns speaking. Daniel spoke how his crime and incarceration hurt his mother. John reflected on how he went from an illiterate thug to a respected literacy tutor. Paul opened up about his crime and catalogued everyone in the community that he hurt. Everyone in the audience grieved with a mother who told the story of her son's murder. At the end of the day, the organizers encouraged both the incarcerated and community participants to sign a "Responsibility Pledge," a commitment to living a responsible life.[22]

These event organizers were all men who faced many years in prison. They owned up to their crimes. They valued family relationships. Through prison programs and their own individual efforts, they did what was needed to transcend their crime. They were "experts" in offender justice needs.

> *"I am being punished for something I did, but I'm not being allowed to try to do something about it."*[23]

The criminal-justice system focuses on punishing the offending individual. However, it does little to address that person's specific needs. Those who offend are tempted to protect and defend themselves from the blame and punishment of the court. They are largely silenced; attorneys often talk on their behalf. They have little opportunity to show regret or anger, lest those feelings ruin a defense. Even the media often reduces offenders to "animals," void of emotion.

At sentencing, offenders "take" their punishment and "get" what they deserve. This passivity does not promote accountability. The person who offends rarely hears or sees the crime's impact. Even if someone is aware of damages, there are few opportunities to offer repair.

Despite society's expectations, prison often creates more barriers than opportunities for true accountability. Prisoners are physically and emotionally separated from both their families and the broader community. This separation breeds blindness to the crime's harms and blocks most efforts for repair.

The prison environment impacts the prisoner personally as well. The separation sends the message that the incarcerated are worthless. Even when intending to create responsible community members, prisons take away responsibility through constant control. Prisons effectively silence prisoners by minimizing their humanity. In this environment many prisoners struggle for respect, defending themselves against anything that threatens that need for respect. While some incarcerated individuals rise above prison, many others find it hard to soul-search for personal healing, let alone face their crime and take responsibility for it

The criminal-justice system frequently focuses on only one aspect of individuals—their offending—and ignores the many other aspects, including their strengths. Moreover, it freezes offending individuals in time. People who commit crimes remain "offenders." Even terms like "ex-offender" or "former prisoner" limit one's humanity. Many social policies—for instance, the loss of voting rights and discriminatory employment requirements—suggest that those who offend "need not apply" for community life.

Restorative justice attempts to do justice in a way that promotes real accountability to the victim and personal healing. The eight justice needs show a way to do that.

Offender justice needs

People who offend need both *relationship* and *safety* if expected to deal with a crime's impacts and causes. Healthy relationships provide the support and encouragement needed to work for accountability and healing. Safety makes it possible for the offending individual to make him or herself vulnerable without fear of shame or judgment.

At times, an offender may need to temporarily leave the broader community for safety reasons. Even during these times of separation, offending individuals require access to safe and meaningful relationships, especially with family. And, the place to which they go must do no further harm to them. A "do-no-harm" environment embodies respect, care,

> *"It is dangerous in prison. You have to choose to hang out with people who will not pull you down and cause you trouble."*[24]

> *"Programs can't rehabilitate; you have to rehabilitate yourself."*[25]

trust, and humility while promoting accountability and healing.

Offending individuals face dual responsibilities of accountability and personal healing. In order to meet these obligations in a meaningful way, offenders need a say in how to fulfill them. Through personal empowerment, the offending individual no longer "takes his/her punishment." Rather, he or she actively participates in the search for understanding and justice. While drawing on a person's inner abilities, this empowerment requires guidance from others to ensure that all justice participants' needs are met in the process.

Accountability is the process of "making things right" in a way that directly relates to the crime and the people hurt by it. It includes the following:

Elements of accountability

1. Admitting one's choice to commit the crime and accepting that the victim is neither responsible for the crime nor the sentence;
2. Understanding how the crime hurt others and owning up to one's responsibility for those damages;
3. Taking steps to repair those harms.

Accountability extends to the three other justice participants—victims, offender families, and the community.

> *"There is no way to rationalize any part of my crime."*[26]

"I would just hope that by the way I spend the rest of my life, whether it's in prison or not, [my victim's family] could in some way see that I do understand what I did and that I'm trying to change other people's lives. I hope in some way it makes up for my irresponsibility before."[27]

Accountability requires a full understanding of the crime and its impacts on the victim. There is no one way to gain this understanding. It may come through talking with the victim, reading an impact-of-crime statement, or listening to other victims share their stories. It may come in part by coming to understand one's own experiences of victimization.

Crime impacts people in different ways, so repairing the harm may vary from person to person and situation to situation. Discovering how to repair the harm often requires some sort of information exchange between the offender and victim or victim's representatives. Restitution is an important way to make things right.

Storytelling and venting feelings have a role in both accountability and healing. Admitting to the crime requires offenders to speak to what they did. In doing so, they also reflect on what they were feeling before, during, and after the crime. In doing so offenders gain a better understanding of the impacts of their crime and what they can do about it.

When offenders tell their stories and feelings, the focus turns to the crime's causes, to times when offenders may have been victimized before and after the crime, and to the

"I'm still a person that is driven, an assertive person. I still believe in causes, but now my causes are positive as opposed to being negative . . . I get high off accomplishments."[28]

> *"I couldn't love myself until I forgave myself. I couldn't change until then."*[29]

crime's impact on themselves. When these stories are spoken and heard, the offender experiences validation, making it easier for that person to work toward personal healing.

Those who offend seek *information* to understand the crime and justice response. Some of these questions are practical and legal. What happens in court? What is the best defense? Will I go to prison? If I do, what happens with my family? Will I get out? Other questions are philosophical and spiritual. Why did I do it? How did I get to this place in my life? What does this all say about me as a person? What does the crime and sentence mean for my life? How do I make a life in prison? The journey toward meaning requires the ability to seek answers to these questions.

Individuals choose if and when they want to experience personal *growth*. It requires them to remove the cloak of offending and turn toward their inner, true self. For some, experiencing growth comes before accountability. For others, meaningful accountability triggers growth.

I have heard incarcerated men and women talk about three key growth areas. First, they deal with those times when they were victims themselves or hurt by another per-

> *"I passed my GED . . . It made me feel wonderful. It was the first time I had the opportunity to make my family proud of me . . . But more than that, it allowed me to see what I was capable of as an individual."*[30]

"I'm a man who has come to grips with himself and the world around him. I understand that I am only here for a while, and that I should try to make the world a better place than it was when I came here. I feel remorse for the things I've done in my life, and I want to try to make it up to the people that I've done it to and to society as a whole."[31]

son. Second, they return to healthy values and live by those values in all areas of their lives. Finally, they acquire the skills and education necessary to lead a full life in the community.

Fulfilling the preceding needs results in personal *meaning*. Meaning places the offending individual back into the web of relationships. That person transcends the experience and label of "offender." Some incarcerated individuals refer to this experience as "becoming the person I am meant to be." They once again (or for the first time) are able to fully participate in a purposeful life.

Restorative justice respects the humanity of those who offend. The philosophy also creates a way to promote accountability and personal healing at the same time. In doing so, the offending individual receives support to "make things right" not only for others, but for themselves as well. As those who offend heal, so does the community. The web of relationships becomes stronger.

9. Reconnecting Offenders' Families

Tara and her mother, Liz, had a good relationship during the years of Tara's incarceration. Yet, when faced with Tara's pending release, they knew they had avoided some important issues about what things would be like when she returned home. In particular, they never talked openly about their mutual desire for Tara to live with Liz. They both had concerns and apprehension about what this living arrangement would be like. How will Tara respect her mother's place? How will Liz respect that her daughter is now an adult? How will they make sure they don't offend each other?

With the help of Mary, who facilitates Transitional Conferencing sessions and who Tara knew through a prison program, the mother and daughter met to find answers to these and other questions. By the end of the conversation, Liz and Tara made agreements about how to live together and deal with time and space issues. Liz commented at the end of the meeting that, though exhausted, she was energized and feeling positive about Tara's return home.[32]

Liz is profoundly impacted by the crime her child committed. Yet, she and other families like hers are rarely noticed by the criminal-justice system. Family needs represent a unique relationship between the offending loved one, the victim, and the community. These needs become even

> *"The family is doing time. He might be paying [for his crime] but I don't think as dearly as the family is."*[33]

more complex when the offender's family is the direct crime victim.

Offender families are in a vulnerable position. They experience the crime's financial impact when, for instance, they hire attorneys, miss work to attend court, or lose a breadwinner to prison. The community often blames and judges the family. The media frequently treat family members as only a "story" and go to great lengths for that story. Many family members are reduced to simply the "offender's mother" or "offender's brother." The family carries the stigma of offending.

All the while, family members try to make sense of their own reactions. Their feelings can range from love or guilt to anger and resentment. They may struggle with their own feelings of accountability and a desire to make amends on behalf of their loved one. For some, the crime permanently breaks the family bond. Other families rally around and support their loved one. The relationship with the loved one, even when broken, remains central to the family experience. These conflicting and varied reactions may occur even when the family is the victim.

The criminal-justice system ignores families and offers little to meet their needs. The justice process is a lonely and confusing one. Families often have limited, and frequently very controlled, access to their loved one. The family struggles to maintain relationships when their loved one is sentenced to prison. There are few opportunities for families to interact with victims, if desired. When family is the victim, their experiences are similar to those of the other crime victims. Familial healing is difficult with this justice experience.

Restorative justice has not traditionally included offender families as a justice participant. Yet they have the same eight justice needs as their loved one. The remainder of this chapter explores family needs in three parts. The first part presents an overview of family justice needs with the assumption that the family is *not* the crime victim. The second part explores the relationship between the family and the crime victim. The final part briefly discusses families who *are* the direct crime victims.

Family justice needs

Families need recognition that they are impacted by the crime. The resulting need for *relationship* and *safety* involves both the community and the offending loved one. Families deserve caring and welcoming support from the community. Safe community relationships refrain from judging, blaming, or hurting the family, and instead provide validation and respect.

Families (adults and children alike) need the chance to figure out and maintain trusting, honest, and empathetic relationships with the offending member. Families also carry concern for their loved one's well-being in prison and seek opportunities to ensure his or her safety.

Children, in particular, need to feel love and support. Because parent-child relationships are difficult from prison, children need special attention as they learn how to relate from a distance and in a prison visiting room. These

> *"He's made a home for himself in prison. It's the ones on the outside that can't make a home."*[34]

> *"My child was so scared to tell his mom how angry and scared he was."*[35]

relationships are made more difficult when children are put in the middle of parental conflicts.

Empowerment goes hand-in-hand with safe relationships. Families need the chance to make decisions about their relationships and how to make them work. This control is often absent, especially when a loved one is in prison. Families are at the mercy of policies that create barriers to relationships. However, when empowered to do so, families can create and maintain healthy relationships.

Empowerment also extends to participation in the justice process. The offender family had little, if any, control over their loved one's actions. Regaining control requires helping the family to make decisions that affect them. In addition, because of the family-offender relationship, families need the chance to participate in determining how their loved one will be accountable to all those impacted by the crime, and how the offender will get his or her other needs met.

Dealing with the crime requires that families face a dual identity as family members and as persons impacted by the crime. The necessary *venting of feelings and storytelling* are, then, unique and diverse. The family tries to make sense of the crime's impacts and their personal reactions. And the family strives to understand their loved one and what the crime means for the family unit.

> *"I resent keeping the kids because my life is turned completely around."*[36]

> *"I didn't know what was happening right from the moment he was arrested. I didn't know what to do until it was too late."*[37]

Family members feel many different, and even conflicting, feelings including anger, bitterness, love, compassion, confusion, and fear. A family may have all these feelings toward the offending loved one. A family may also feel empathy and accountability toward the victim. Children need to understand that all these feelings are normal.

The stories that accompany these feelings may relate to the crime, incarceration and its effects, and even family life before and after the crime. The ability to share feelings and stories requires meaningful communication, which is often difficult when a loved one is in prison. Family members may even desire to talk with and express their feelings to the victim.

The family's dual role creates a diverse set of *information* needs. Families have "what," "why," and "how" questions regarding the crime. They also have questions that are personal and introspective. Why am I reacting the way I am? What does the crime say about me? What does this mean for the family? Other questions show concern for the offending loved one. What will happen to him or her? Will s/he be safe? How can I help him or her? What can I do to make up for what my loved one did? These questions are practical, relational, and spiritual all at the same time.

Children seek their own information. Perhaps most importantly, they want to know that their parent loves and thinks about them. For children who have seen a lot of crime, they often wonder if crime is okay. Children of incarcerated parents have concerns about the parent's safety and life in prison and about when a parent returns home. Their questions require honest, realistic answers that are age-appropriate. They may need an adult's help to dispel fear and expose myths about prison, without glamorizing prison or crime. This information helps children feel more secure.

Crime creates the chance for familial *growth*. Because offender and family needs overlap, growth requires mutual, committed, and consistent relationships. During this time of growth, families can tend to their relationships by affirming strong bonds and mending the broken ones, while addressing the crime's impacts and causes.

This work on relationships challenges family members to cut through denial about the crime and sentence. They need to name values and talk about how people are going to get along. Family members may create boundaries. Especially with an incarcerated loved one, family roles may change. For instance, grandmother becomes mother. The spouse who remains home grows more independent as they take on new responsibilities. Growth means figuring out these new roles and relationships.

A child's personal growth helps prevent future offending and incarceration. Successful growth requires that parents (even if they are not together) and guardians make a shared commitment to love and care for the child.

Like growth, *accountability* is a mutual, two-way street between offender and family. The offending loved one admits that his or her actions were a choice, faces up to how the crime impacted the family, and actively makes things right

> *"I learned I could be happy, even though my dad was in prison."*[38]

> *"I have a couple of friends now, their moms use drugs, and we can sit down and have a conversation about it. It helps us just to realize that we're not alone and that we can still do what we're put here to do, 'cause I feel everyone was put here for a reason."*[39]

with them. A family's accountability requires the same but deals with offending within the family unit. This accountability begins to address possible familial causes of crime.

Families change when faced with crime. Meeting these justice needs helps a family to adapt and move forward. Just like individuals, a family establishes a new understanding of who they are. Members also gain new understanding about who they are as individuals within the family unit. They find *meaning*.

With attention to their justice needs, offender families move along their own healing journeys toward meaning. In doing so, they support their offending loved one on his or her own journey. Restorative justice offers a way to respect offender families and build them back into community with others. In doing so, the web of relationships strengthens.

Family and the crime victim

While the family may not share responsibility for their family member's offending, many families feel an obligation to the victim and a desire to make amends on their loved one's behalf. Azim Khamisa and Ples Felix, whose story was briefly told on p.12, are examples of what can happen through the family-victim relationship. This relationship brings additional meaning to the eight justice needs.

The family may carry a sense of obligation to acknowledge the harm their loved one caused to the victim. While the family did not commit the crime, they may acutely feel the harm it caused. They are an important resource in helping their loved one to understand the impact of the crime and help to make things right. The offender's family's own acknowledgment of the harm, publicly or privately, can also serve to vindicate the victim, an important victim need. Whether simply encouraging their offending member or actively helping to make amends, the family promotes justice and victim reparation.

A family's concern for accountability and the victim suggest that the family's needs may correspond to the victim's needs. For instance, a family may wish to talk about their concern for the victim. They may feel the need to make apologies and statements of responsibility on their loved one's behalf. They may have questions for the victim or wish to answer the victim's questions. They may want to ensure safety—their own, in response to concerns with retaliation, and that of the victim, in response to their loved one's actions. Not all families feel this connection to the victim but when they do, they usually have to find their own ways to live it out since their needs are not addressed by the justice process.

Regardless of whether offenders' families relate directly to victims, the family and victim healing paths often do run parallel and sometimes cross.

When family is the crime victim

Some individuals commit crimes against their own families. When a family member is the crime victim, it impacts the family in complex ways. Their resulting needs are a combination of those of victims and offender families. If your family is your victim, I suggest you read the victim chapter (Chapter 7) after reading this chapter.

Suzette's son killed a man in a hit-and-run crash. Suzette learned later that the man was a white priest. Her thoughts turned to the reality that her son was black. She thought to herself, "They're gonna hang him alive. He has two black marks against him—not only is the man he killed Caucasian, but he is a priest." Suzette called her prayer intercessor. She asked this woman to pray for the victim's family first and then pray for her son and then her.

Suzette was alone at her son's sentencing. She was afraid when she saw all the victim's family members in attendance. She didn't know how they'd react. Suzette also heard the family read a statement supporting a light sentence for her son. They didn't want revenge. They wanted to honor the values for which their brother stood and his work with delinquent boys.

When Suzette conveyed her thanks and condolences to the family through the District Attorney, the attorney said the family wanted to meet her and had been praying for her. There, outside the courtroom, Suzette and the victim's family prayed together. Suzette reflects that "there is no way to express the power of this kind of forgiveness and compassion. These people, who had just lost their brother, were sent by divine messenger to help me keep my own heart open. This was an act of great redemption."[40]

This combination contributes to confusing and sometimes conflicting reactions. Sometimes a family's needs as victims take priority over their needs as family members of the offender. Safety may require that family members remain apart, at least temporarily. Relationships may continue but with clear boundaries, or they may cease to exist. Accountability is required, even if the family will not be together again as a unit. Individuals who have offended against their families show respect by recognizing that their family members are crime victims and by demonstrating accountability to them.

This chapter merely scratches the surface of an offender family's experiences and needs. More exploration is required to fully understand how families fit into the restorative-justice philosophy and its practices. At any rate, as this exploration continues, it is important to remember offender families when doing justice.

10. Restorative-Justice Practices

Restorative justice is a *philosophy*. It can be *practiced* in many different ways. Restorative practices vary by who is included and how those individuals' needs are met. Even so, restorative practices share a commitment to each justice participant and promote both accountability and healing. Values of respect, care, trust, and humility prevail. Ultimately, restorative practices seek to repair the web. This chapter presents a framework for understanding five common practices.

Restorative practices

There are several ways to understand restorative justice. One way is to look at how many restorative elements are used in a particular practice. Some practices may use more elements and thus may be closer to fully restorative than others. Another way is to look at the different levels at which the practice occurs—individually, relationally, or socially.

Restorative practices honor justice participants by:

- Respecting their needs.
- Promoting accountability and healing.
- Practicing respect, trust, care, and humility.
- Rebuilding the web.

LEVELS OF RESTORATIVE PRACTICE

1. **Socially Restorative**
2. **Relationally Restorative**
3. **Individually Restorative**

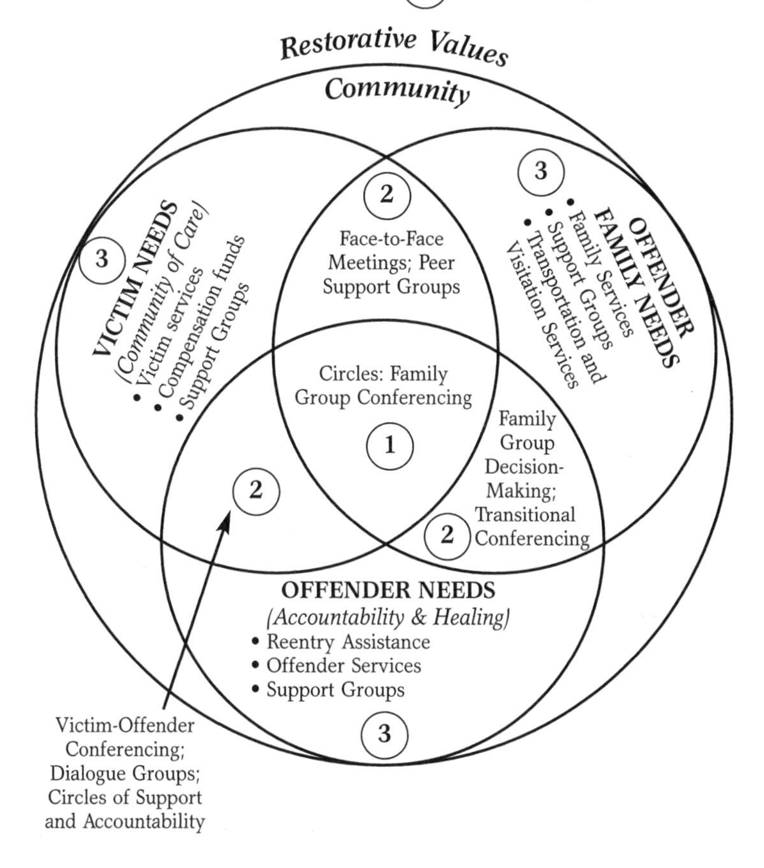

The diagram above offers a way to understand different levels of practices. The center of the diagram, where the three circles intersect, are practices or programs that are *socially restorative* (1). These practices not only respond to the needs of all the justice participants in one justice response, but also create the opportunity to deal with broader social issues related to the crime. Just outside the center are examples of practices that are *relationally restorative* (2). These practices respond to the overlapping needs of two intersecting sets of justice participants. The outer parts of the circles represent *individually restorative practices* (3). These practices focus solely on those individual justice needs that don't involve interaction with other justice participant needs.

Many of the practices at the center of this diagram—the socially and the relationally restorative practices—bring people, including community members, together to talk about what happened and what needs to be done. However, restorative practices do not necessarily require face-to-face conversations. What is required, at a minimum, is that all justice participant needs and issues are addressed using restorative principles and values in that one practice.

The outermost rim of the diagram represents the community. The community surrounds each of the three justice participant circles, symbolizing its support and accountability. It also represents the community as an important partner, and sometimes participant, in each practice. The connections between the community and the inner circles also represent advocacy. That is, it represents the community taking seriously its relationships with each justice participant to promote system and community change.

Restorative principles and values surround the community. Community relates to the participants and processes based on these principles and values. And by extension, all the practices inside the circle, even individually restorative ones, are guided by restorative principles and values. A fully restorative-justice system would require that all restorative practices be in use.

This model highlights just a few common restorative practices. As the case studies in this book suggest, there are many creative ways to apply restorative-justice values and to meet justice participant needs. The remainder of this chapter explores several of the most common practices and introduces the idea of a restorative system.

Face-to-face meetings

Face-to-face meetings between the justice participants are the most common restorative practices.[41] While not the right choice for everyone, those who choose to meet usually find these encounters both satisfying and powerful.

A facilitator assists each justice participant in deciding if a meeting is right for him or her. The facilitator explains the process, answers questions, and talks about the participant's goals, hopes, and concerns about meeting. All the while, the facilitator shows equal concern and care for all participants.

> The facilitator shows equal concern and care for all participants.

If each justice participant wants to meet, the facilitator prepares them to come together. This preparation further explores participants' goals, what each would like to say and hear, needs for safety, and the specific process to be used.

The facilitator leads the meeting. In this role, the facilitator 1) creates a safe meeting atmosphere, 2) supports the participants as they say what they need to say, 3) shows respect for everyone present, and 4) assists the participants in achieving their goals. The facilitator's role is best understood as a quiet, yet actively engaged, witness. The participants ultimately own the meeting.

While there are some differences, this general process for selecting, preparing, and leading a meeting is similar across models. I explore Circles, Family Group Conferences, and Victim-Offender Conferencing in more detail below.

Circles

High for days, George, 17, was arrested for drug possession when he drove his car off the road. He sat in Circle with the community to deal with his charges. George said little as they expressed their anger with his drug use and dangerous driving. Finally, George said, "I don't care about death. Dying doesn't bother me. I just care about having as much fun as possible."

The conversation suddenly changed. The Circle members remembered feeling the same way as teens and hearing similar things from their own children. This indifference to life became the focus of the sentence. The Circle, including George, agreed that he would complete a hospice training course to learn to care for dying people.[42]

Circles bring together all justice participants, including members of the broader community, to deal with a crime. While seated in a Circle, each participant talks about the crime from his or her perspective. The Circle members then together create a plan for the offending member to make amends to the victim and community and to address the crime's causes.

A "keeper" facilitates and participates in the Circle. This individual passes a talking piece around the Circle as a symbolic tool that promotes both listening and speaking. Circle members speak only when they hold the piece. And, the piece keeps moving around the Circle until the participants say all they have to say. The time and commitment to the process promotes respect for participants' relationships, including their differences and commonalities. This respect, in turn, promotes completion of the plan.

Family Group Conferences

A teen assaulted and stole money from his grandmother. New to the country and without support systems, the grandmother was concerned about the bills that now would not get paid. The teen, supported by a teacher and refugee organization, and the grandmother, supported by a victim organization, met together. In their native language, the meeting opened with a prayer and continued with both family members telling their stories of what happened.

While the grandmother told her story, her grandchild got tears in his eyes. The grandchild told of experiences in a refugee camp and the pressures of adjusting to life in the new country. Both family members felt the same way. They reached an agreement that the grandchild would repay all the money, live separate from his grandmother until she felt safe, get counseling, do community work, and attend school. A mentor from his own culture agreed to follow up to make sure he met his obligations. Not only were these obligations met but both he and his grandmother formed new support networks in the community.[43]

Family Group Conferences (FGCs) bring together the offender, his or her family, and the victim and their family or supporters. If appropriate, others may be included, such as representatives from community organizations and police. After each participant talks about what happened, the offender and family meet privately to create a plan for dealing with the crime. The family presents the plan to the other participants and, together, they modify and finalize it.

Most often used with youth, FGCs operate under the premise that the family is an "expert" in the crime, particularly its causes and ways to respond, but also that the family needs to be empowered to respond. In an FGC, the family is able to deal with both familial causes of crime and its impacts. The conference process empowers families to work on their relationships and build internal resources that, with help from the community, assist with completion of the FGC plan.

Victim-Offender Conferencing

A young couple was murdered by a friend and an accomplice. The mothers of the deceased grew close in the aftermath. Both were interested in meeting with one of the offenders. One mother wanted to find out the truth of what happened. The other mother also wanted truth as well as information about the offender, his family and background, and what he was doing while in prison. She also was considering forgiveness. Though anxious, the offender agreed to meet, with his own mother present for support.

Over several hours, the man and the mothers talked. The mother who was looking for information was satisfied with what he told them. The other mother said what she came to say and found out more about the man. In the process, the victims' mothers were able to see the offender as a real person, rather than as a monster. While the meeting brought back a lot of emotions for him, the offender felt relieved to have talked with the mothers. The offender's mother was also grateful for the experience. She remains supportive of her son and responsive to the mothers' needs.[44]

Victim-Offender Conferencing, also known as Victim-Offender Dialogue or Mediation, brings the victim and offender together to talk about the crime. Each may bring support people, if desired. Some Conferencing approaches focus solely on the dialogue. Others promote restitution agreements. Still others let the victim and offender decide the focus. Regardless of the approach, Conferencing is about the offender, victim, and each of their individual needs.

There is great diversity among Conferencing programs. Some programs work only with juvenile offenders, others only with adults. Some focus on violent crime, others on nonviolent. Some meetings occur within hours of a crime, and others years later.

Conferencing can be victim initiated or offender initiated. It may be used instead of a court process, or as the sentencing phase of a criminal-justice process. Some Conferences occur while the offending individual is in prison or on parole. This diversity makes it possible to create programs in a variety of settings.

Dialogue groups

Seated with a group of prisoners and outside volunteers, Bob and Kathy told of the murder of their three children by a drunk driver. They passed photos of their children and of the wrecked car, telling of their pain and struggle with revenge, justice, forgiveness, and love. The rest of the group listened, visibly shaken. Over the following few weeks, in small groups including both prisoners and outsiders, each took turns telling his or her own personal stories. They talked of robberies and murders and drug-dealing and addictions. They discussed shared emotions—greed, violence, isolation, courage, love, and hope. They soul-searched together. Each session ended as participants offered a closing reflection.[45]

Dialogue groups bring together "unrelated" victims, offenders, and community members. Facilitators plan and guide storytelling and dialogue on such topics as offending, victimization, justice, restitution, forgiveness, and reconciliation. This practice is most commonly used in prison.

Even though participants do not have a specific crime in common, dialogue groups offer a way to meet justice participant needs. Participants talk about their crime stories and, in return, receive validation for their experiences and feelings. Offending participants talk of their remorse and responsibility, offering symbolic vindication to victim participants. They learn about crime's impacts and causes. Participants receive many of the same benefits of face-to-face meetings.

Dialogue-group participants commit to learning from and understanding each other. First seen as simply "victims" and "offenders," participants often find they share similar hopes, dreams, pain, and joy. They may develop compassion and mutual care for each other. The dialogue also inspires hope for community change. Some groups even create plans to work together on justice-related projects.

Group structure varies across programs. Groups may use Circles, small- and large-group discussion, group activities, and victim panels. Others use art or writing exercises, workbooks, and written discussion guides. Groups may hold four to twelve sessions over weeks or months. While many groups are held inside prisons, others occur in the community. This flexibility makes it possible to design programs that meet a variety of needs and attract a variety of people.

Circles of Support and Accountability

Two years before her release from prison, Jade felt she needed support to go back into the community. She requested a Circle. Her Circle of three trained volunteers met every Wednesday in the prison. As they laughed and cried together, they got to know each other and became trusted companions.

Upon Jade's release, the Circle rallied around her. They took her to food banks, helped her with a job search, and encouraged her through the difficult times. Jade has now been in the community for over two-and-a-half years. She has been steadily em-

ployed for two years and has earned several promotions. Her Circle, now together for almost five years, still keeps in touch and offers support when any of them are in need. Now that her life is stabilized and going well, Jade is ready to address some unresolved issues from her past.[46]

Circles of Support and Accountability (CSA) link people leaving prison with volunteers who offer support in the transition back to community life. The CSA also responds to community and victim needs, thus adding the element of accountability. To this end, community members and victims or victim representatives participate in the Circle.

The CSA consists of the offender, called the "core member," and a small group of trained community members. The CSA begins to meet when the core member is still in prison. Upon release, the Circle continues to meet regularly, often weekly. Some Circles stay together for many years.

In the meetings, the Circle talks about how things are going, successes and obstacles, and the core member's needs. They work together to solve problems. The Circle assists the core member as he or she meets practical needs and builds new relationships. As Jade's story shows, the Circle members are actively involved in the core member's daily life. The CSA may also advocate on the core member's behalf within the community.

The CSA commits to open, empowering, and trustworthy interactions. In doing so, the Circle models healthy and responsible community life. The Circle also promotes accountability to victims and the community. For instance, the Circle helps the core member avoid situations in which they may be at risk of re-offending. While the core member's actual victim and community are not necessarily involved, the CSA still attends to their interests.

A restorative system

Many of these restorative practices exist alongside or within the criminal-justice system. For instance, Victim-Offender Mediation is sometimes used to divert juvenile offenders from the system. Circles have been used to create a sentence, including sentences that keep people out of prison. Studies show that justice participants, especially victims and offenders, experience increased satisfaction with the justice process when restorative practices are used.

However, a criminal-justice system that simply offers restorative practices is different from a *restorative-justice system.* A restorative-justice system would be built, from the ground up, on the web principles and restorative beliefs and values. Restorative practices would not be simply an "add-on" but would be central to the process.

Such a system would look and feel quite different to the justice participants. Right from the moment of arrest, justice would start with the harms experienced by victims. Every aspect of the justice process would promote offender accountability and healing. Offender families would be invited to stand with their loved one as they took steps to repair the harm. Everything in the system would be designed to respect individuals, restore relationships, and promote the common good.

No such fully-restorative system currently exists today, although the implications and possibilities are being discussed in a variety of communities. The youth justice system of New Zealand probably comes the closest to a restorative system in its design. When used as intended, serious offenses by young people in New Zealand are addressed in restorative conferences rather than in court, with the court serving as a backup.[47]

11. Restorative Practices, Justice, and Prison

Meeting over nine weeks, a group of incarcerated women sit in a Circle on a journey toward healing. To be part of this Circle, the women have accepted responsibility for their crimes and are prepared to talk openly about it with the other Circle members. It is not easy and many doubt that they can do it. Yet, using a talking piece, each woman speaks to her crime experience. She considers what her victim may want to say to her and what she would like to say in return.

The women explore together experiences with personal change, healing, and kindness, sharing in ways they have never done before. They find themselves rebuilding relationships and apologizing for past conflicts with each other. The women begin to take ownership of opening and closing the Circle, bringing their own reflections to share with the group. The women, some initially doubters, agreed that the Circle was one of the best things to happen to them. They now dream of using Circles to deal with conflicts within prison and to respond to family issues.[48]

Many current restorative practices have originated within communities outside prison. Often, when restorative practices are used in prison, they're initiated by

> ***If you may not contact your victim:***
>
> - Pay your restitution.
> - Take programs.
> - Write a letter to yourself taking responsibility.
> - Donate to victim groups.
> - Help victims you know.
> - Take part in victim impact or dialogue groups.

people from the outside. This reality has left many people in prison questioning whether restorative practices are really available to them. If their role is limited to waiting for someone else to offer practices, people in prison become passive recipients of restorative justice.

This chapter introduces ways that incarcerated women and men can initiate restorative practices in prison by working with existing programs both within the prison and on the outside. The chapter ends by exploring the limits of restorative practices in prison and the idea of "restorative spaces."

Contacting existing programs

Many incarcerated individuals wish to meet with their victims. Others desire to start a restorative program. Prisoners may achieve both goals by requesting services from existing programs.

Requesting a meeting with one's victim carries benefits and risks to both the offender and victim. Skilled practitioners and existing programs can offer the safest way to request these meetings. Prior to making contact, consider the following questions:

1. What do you hope to get out of a meeting?
2. What will it be like if your hopes are not met?

3. What will it be like if the victim does not want to talk to you?
4. What do you expect of the victim (e.g. forgiveness)?
5. Are those expectations fair and just?

The meeting facilitator will determine, based on many factors, whether to contact the victim.

Some incarcerated individuals find that policies and rules prohibit them from contacting their victims, even through existing programs. These rules often reflect the concern for victim safety and the risk of revictimization. In such situations, the offender can find symbolic and creative ways to take responsibility and make amends.

People in prison can also take leadership in creating restorative practices that serve prisoners, among others. By inviting community organizations and prison officials to join with them, incarcerated individuals can create partnerships to develop dialogue groups, Circles of Support and Accountability, and even victim-offender dialogue programs. People in prison do not need to wait for others to do the work. Admittedly there are obstacles to overcome, but with imagination and persistence, with a sound proposal and allies, people in prison can get things started.[49]

To find restorative allies, practitioners, and programs:

- Talk to prison staff and to other prisoners.
- Write to offender, victim, and mediation agencies.
- Search the Web, or ask someone on the outside to do it for you.
- Research books, magazines, and videos.
- Ask an out-of-state program for a local referral.

Use restorative practices to deal with:

- Conflicts involving both prisoners and staff.
- Crimes that happen in prison.
- Family relationships and conflicts.
- Disciplinary infractions.

Using restorative practices in prison

Prison is a community in and of itself. As such, restorative practices can be used to deal with crime and conflict inside prison. Some suggest that the violence and conflict in prison grow out of the lack of healing justice for crime. If so, this is all the more reason to use restorative justice inside the prison walls.

Conflict is common in prison. Prisoners clash with each other and with staff. Staff have conflicts with staff. Circles can respond to conflict involving a whole prison block or an administrative department. Mediation can assist with disputing cellmates or co-workers. Restorative practices provide responses to countless other social conflicts.

Prison-based crime creates the same justice participants as identified in this book. The full range of restorative practices can be used to address the resulting eight justice needs, so that victims in prison have access to the same basic services as victims on the outside.

Restorative practices can serve prisoners and their families. A Family Group Conference can bring families together to make agreements about child care. The same process can assist families in preparing for a loved one's return home. Conferencing is useful for resolving specific and familial conflicts that may arise during the sentence.

Restorative practices provide alternatives to punishment-oriented responses to rule-breaking. Circles promote an understanding of the causes and effects of rule-breaking, and even the source of rules. Disciplinary decisions could be made in a Family Group Conference, inviting the family to talk about the impact of rule-breaking on them. Both processes actively engage the rule-breaker in creating the disciplinary response.[50]

Incarcerated individuals can provide leadership in proposing and developing these types of programs in prison. The allies and practitioners of crime-specific programs in the community can be mobilized to assist prison programs. As well, prisoners can use these practices informally. For instance, they can use a Circle process in meetings or offer to help people in conflict talk to each other.

Restorative "spaces"

Using restorative practices in prison brings a healing element to prison and to those who live and work within it. Yet, a prison that uses such practices is not a "restorative prison." In reality, there is no such thing. To be fully restorative, prison would offer more than restorative practices. It would also transform its goals, values, culture, and even architecture. A restorative transformation would radically alter the image and experience of prison. Prison would likely no longer be "prison" as we know it. Restorative-justice practice in prison includes transforming the foundation and role of prison, and possibly even replacing the existence of it.

I use the language of "restorative spaces" to label those places built on a restorative foundation. An image for restorative spaces is a "do-no-harm room," a room in which offenders feel safe to take responsibility for their crime and experience healing. When a group of incarcerated men were asked to imagine what such a room would look like, they drew a place decorated and furnished with such things as ethics books, telephones, comfortable chairs, doors and windows, music, an aquarium, plants, and a mountain view. Their room symbolized restorative values like respect, relationship, safety, comfort, communication, hope, and life. Words like "sanctuary" or "refuge," used in trauma-healing work, also suggest the nature of a restorative space.[51]

These images and words suggest that restorative spaces create a temporary separation between an offender and those impacted by his or her actions. At the same time the offender stays connected to key relationships that help meet the justice needs of the various justice participants. This can be achieved through, for example, physical locations embedded in an offender's community that use the surrounding relationships to promote healing and accountability. However, these spaces are not limited to physical locations. They may

Restorative places promote:

- Respect, care, trust, and humility
- Relationship with others
- Personal healing
- Safety
- Accountability
- Self-worth and personal power
- Mutual responsibility
- Independence, productivity, and constructiveness
- Understanding and acceptance
- Creativity and positivity
- Connection to nature and spirituality
- Responsible decision-making
- Honesty and openness
- Kindness and love
- Nonviolence

also be relational or emotional in nature. For instance, a restorative space may involve encircling an offender with safe and strong relationships as a way to address that individual's justice needs. Or, a restorative space may provide a supportive forum in which an offender can heal and strengthen his or her inner self.

There are few, if any, examples of restorative spaces in use instead of prisons. However, there are some promising examples that move toward this vision. For example, some prisons have special cell blocks on which residents commit to living restoratively and participate in restorative programs. Others offer hiking and gardening as a way to nurture spiritual well-being. Still others create special cultural units so prisoners can learn and practice their cultural teachings as part of their path to accountability and healing. And, prison staff who approach their jobs from a restorative framework create restorative environments by nature of their interactions with incarcerated individuals and other staff.

The idea of restoratives spaces suggests that relationships are a means to justice, not something to which one returns after justice or a period of confinement. Subsequently, the meaning and experience of parole and reentry would also change. Because an offender would not have left relationship, the barriers to parole and reentry may disappear. Reentry may even become moot.

Replacing prison with restorative physical, relational, and emotional spaces may seem unlikely. It assumes that society embraces restorative values. This begs the question, then, of how to create a restorative society. I believe such a society begins with the individual. When one person acts restoratively, including in prison, it influences others. The following chapter explores ways to live restoratively toward this end.

12. Restorative Living in Prison

While incarcerated, David attended religious services regularly. One day in the chapel he saw Jose, the man who murdered his brother-in-law. Jose was part of a faith-based program at this same prison. David learned that Jose was also a man of deep faith. He requested a meeting with Jose and saw it as perhaps his only opportunity to find answers to questions he and his sister and niece had carried for years. He saw himself as an ambassador for his family.

Supported by a fellow prisoner, and guided by a trained restorative-justice staff facilitator, David and Jose met to talk about what happened. In that meeting, David carried a message to Jose from his sister, the wife of the man Jose murdered. David told Jose that his sister "believes that forgiveness is a powerful thing and wants you to know that she forgives you for killing her husband." Jose was speechless. He finally said, "I don't know what to do with that . . . I can't find any words . . . . "

After a few minutes he stood up, turned around, and lifted his shirt, revealing a large prison tattoo that stretched across his entire back. It read "UNFORGIVEN." Jose sat back down, simply saying that he had a lot to think about. Following the meeting, both David and Jose reflected on the life-changing experience.[52]

The way that the criminal-justice system functions suggests that people are disposable. Their experiences, feelings, and relationships are not worth attention. Our shared humanity is deemed unimportant. Criminal justice grows out of the broken web of relationships in society and, in turn, perpetuates this brokenness. Could changing the justice system change society? Restorative justice advocates often argue that it could.

Act the way you are *meant* to, not the way you are *expected* to.

Restorative justice offers a way to transform society. If offenders and victims deserve respect, everyone deserves respect. If people impacted by crime are important, everyone in the community is important. Restorative justice promotes social change and a strong web of relationships.

But a restorative-justice system is not the only element in social change. Strengthening or recreating community requires that members commit to restorative-justice principles and values themselves. As such, restorative justice is a way of life.

Restorative living calls people to act as if they already live in the strong web of relationships. Individuals treat others as they want to be treated themselves. They act as the "people they are meant to be," even when faced with disrespect, wrongdoing, or harm. For those who believe in the philosophy, restorative living is practicing what they preach and walking the talk.

Restorative living in prison—like restorative justice in the larger society—is counter-cultural. Yet, choosing to live restoratively has the potential to influence others in prison and the culture of prison itself. These changes inside, in turn, can influence the community outside. There are many people

Personal benefits of restorative living

- Inner peace and freedom
- Personal power
- Strength through safe relationships
- Strong inner identity
- Separation from prison "drama"
- Respect

in prison who create the community they want within the prison walls. Many of these same individuals have reached outside the walls through jobs, committees, personal life, and education to transform individuals and their communities.

This chapter discusses six traits of restorative living in prison and the importance of this type of life for the good of all society.

1. Get on the "healing path"

Too often, people do not treat themselves with respect and kindness. Restorative living requires taking care of oneself and getting on the "healing path." While on this path, one looks at one's life, where one has been, and where one wants to go, and then does what is necessary to move toward personal hope and purpose.

A healing person faces and deals with painful experiences and lets go of those things that hold him or her back. It might mean letting go of shame, blame, or excuses for past experiences and belief systems that support the "tough-guy" image and strength through violence.

Healing does not mean weakness. Nor does it imply opening oneself to potential harm. Rather, an individual stands up for him or herself in a way that recognizes the humanity in the other.

Ideas for getting on the healing path

- Treat yourself with respect and see your own worth and goodness.
- Find your personal inner power and take control of your life.
- Accept responsibility for your crime and other behaviors.
- Deal with times you have been a victim and hurt by others.
- Find safe and supportive relationships.
- Face your feelings and get them out.
- See hate and unresolved anger as destructive powers.
- Explore spirituality and forgiveness, including self-forgiveness.

2. Embrace restorative values

Every day, people have countless chances to relate to others—on the job, at school, in the chow line, on the block, during committee meeting, and in visits with family and friends. Each interaction challenges an individual to embrace and use the restorative values of *respect, care, trust,* and *humility*.

Respect requires an individual commitment to listen to, understand, and validate other people, even those one dislikes. An individual demonstrates *care* when she or he accepts the idea of mutual responsibility with others. One who lives with *trust* is not only honest but also brings out the best in others. *Humility* expects that an individual admits his or her mistakes and asks for help when needed. Ultimately, a life guided by restorative values is free of violence, fear, and manipulation.

Ideas for practicing restorative values

- Listen more, talk less.
- Practice random acts of kindness.
- Refrain from gossiping, personal politics, hidden agendas, and backstabbing.
- Be a collaborative leader.
- Take the high road and give people the benefit of the doubt.
- Practice nonviolence.

Practicing restorative values extends to justice professionals and prison staff. As fellow humans, justice and correctional staff deserve to be treated with the same respect, care, trust, and humility that one wants for him or herself. Living by restorative values doesn't mean you have to like someone or like what they do. It simply means remembering their shared humanity with you and acting accordingly.

3. Create a "sanctuary"

On a daily basis, incarcerated individuals experience the stress of prison life. Many people create their own personal sanctuaries that offer temporary refuge from prison. These physical and emotional spaces make it possible to cope with the stress of prison in healthy ways, rather than taking it out on oneself or others.

Changing how one reacts to prison life has the potential to transform the whole of prison life for others. With a personal sanctuary, an individual can become a refuge for others. That person is a safe and trustworthy person to which others can turn. He or she models healthy coping and relationships. The impact is felt across the web of prison life.

Ideas for creating a sanctuary

- Draw or imagine a safe and serene place. Pull out the image when you feel wound up.
- Meditate and practice deep breathing.
- Listen to relaxing music with headphones.
- Take advantage of those times when you can be alone.
- Create a mantra (a 7-10 syllable phrase) that, when repeated, calms you.
- Find an object that represents your healing path. Reflect on it for encouragement.

4. Walk with those who offend

People in prison are surrounded by "offenders" every day. Everyone has been convicted of offending others. Some continue to criminally offend while in prison. And, by nature of being human, almost everyone does things, intentionally and unintentionally, that hurt others socially.

Whatever one has done to hurt another, the offender is responsible for facing what he or she did. Whether it is unfairly cutting someone down in a meeting or berating a spouse for missing a visit, the "offender" has to put him or herself back in check. This means practicing humility by admitting that one's actions hurt another, even when there may be misunderstandings about what happened.

People also have the chance to walk with those who have hurt others. For instance, hold someone accountable when he or she lashes out against someone on the block. Stop another from beating up a "gossip." Listen to someone who is angry about a missed visit and help them to write a letter home that doesn't cut the family down.

Ideas for walking with offenders

- Own up to your offenses.
- Admit when your actions have hurt people in your social and family life.
- Find one thing of worth in someone who did you wrong.
- Write an apology letter to someone you hurt socially.
- Take a new, young commit under your wing.
- Walk away from a fight.

5. Walk with victims

Crime victims live inside and outside prison. To walk with victims requires remembering the victim of one's crime and being there for others, including family, if they become crime victims. Because not all harms are criminal, restorative living also includes being there for people when they are hurt by others in noncriminal ways.

Accountability and "being there" overlap. For instance, efforts to "give back" to victims and to the community both make amends and create a community in which others will not be victimized. Listening, without judgment, to a friend who feels disrespected by another helps him or her deal with the personal attack, and it may stop that person from hurting another through retaliation. Donating money or supplies to a local victim-service agency is symbolic restitution and ensures that the agency has the resources to support your family, if ever victimized.

One may not be able to undo his or her crime or other hurtful actions. But "paying it forward"[53] symbolically makes amends and provides support.

Ideas for walking with victims

- Say, "I'm sorry this happened to you."
- Listen without judgment.
- Pay your restitution.
- If a family member becomes a crime victim, connect him/her with a victim service agency.
- Don't retaliate if someone hurts you.
- Pay it forward.

6. Walk with offenders' families

Family is on the mind of most people in prison. Incarcerated individuals have family on the outside and, for some, family members doing time with them. Many create "family" inside prison. Some individuals committed their crime against their families. A centerpiece to restorative living is understanding, building, and maintaining healthy family relationships.

The first step of walking with family is to have a heart-to-heart talk about how the family is impacted by the crime and prison sentence. Listen, even when it's hard. Make commitments to family life now. When ready, one can open up and talk about past family actions that require accountability.

It's also important to relish and enjoy family life. Restorative living includes taking an interest in family life and giving people on the outside freedom to lead fulfilling lives.

It's particularly important to show love for children and offer assurances that they are not to blame for the crime or incarceration. Relationships require regular communication. Write often, even if the child may not be getting the letters. Work to get along with the child's caregiver.

Ideas for walking with offenders' families

- Write an apology letter to your family.
- Send letters, cards, gifts, and money.
- Involve your children, and other family members, in decisions that affect them.
- Refrain from blaming your loved ones if they miss a visit or call.
- Take a class on communication and use the skills with your family.
- Give your family, and yourself, permission to be happy.

* *If your family is your victim, it can be harmful to write, call, or send communication. Remember and respect that they are victims with unique needs for their own healing.*

Restorative living is about being the parent you always wanted and about being the child your parent always dreamed of.

Restorative living for the common good

Restorative justice is a way to do justice that actively includes the people impacted by crime—offenders, victims, their families, and communities. Its goal is to respect and restore each as individuals, repair relationships, and contribute to the common good. A fully restorative justice system that offers a wide range of restorative practices requires substantial social change. This change reflects a return to a strong web of relationships.

I believe that an individual's commitment to restorative justice promotes this social transformation. When an individual lives restoratively, he or she lives in a way that builds relationships and promotes the common good. That approach changes how people relate back. As those relationships influence each other, the web of relationships begins to recreate itself.

This recreation promotes equal, just, and mutually responsible societies. In a restorative society, everyone has access to safety, power, relationships, financial security, healthcare, education, and meaningful opportunities for employment and recreation. People do not commit crimes. There are no more victims.

Yet, one person can't force another person or system to change. There are times when organized advocacy is necessary to encourage transformation. Restorative advocacy occurs when people and organizations committed to restorative justice join together to transform systems, not just individuals or interpersonal relationships. The system transformation they seek respects the experiences and needs of each and every justice participant.

Living the values of restorative justice is an individual choice that has the potential to create a restorative society. It is a challenging road to take, as it expects much of individuals, interpersonal relationships, and society as a whole. But men and women in prison can help to lead the way.

Endnotes

1 For more information about the Pennsylvania Prison Society, see www.prisonsociety.org or write to Pennsylvania Prison Society, 245 N. Broad St., Suite 300, Philadelphia, PA 19107.

2 See David Cayley, *The Expanding Prison* (Cleveland, OH: The Pilgrim Press, 1998), 215-217; and Brian Caldwell, *The Record,* July 8, 2002.

3 See Azim Khamisa, *From Murder to Forgiveness (*Ank Publishing, Inc.: La Jolla, CA, 2002), 90.

4 See Kay Pranis, "Not in My Backyard," *Conciliation Quarterly* (Summer 2001).

5 James Gilligan offers an interesting perspective on "violence as a form of justice" in *Preventing Violence* (New York: Thames and Hudson, Inc., 2001).

6 Howard Zehr, often considered the pioneer of restorative justice, has been influential in framing these questions and those of restorative justice. His groundbreaking work is *Changing Lenses* (Scottdale, PA: Herald Press, 1990/2005). See also *The Little Book of Restorative Justice* (Intercourse, PA: Good Books, 2002).

7 *A Body in Motion,* written and directed by Ingrid De Sanctis, is based on Howard Zehr's book, *Transcending: Reflections of Crime Victims* (Intercourse, PA: Good Books, 2001). The play tour was a project of the Pennsylvania Prison Society.

8 For more information about the Hollow Water experience, see the video *Hollow Water* (National Film Board of Canada) and Rupert Ross, *Returning to the Teachings: Exploring Aboriginal Justice* (New York: Penguin Books, 1996).

9 Two works that explore "hospitality" and "embrace" include Miroslav Volf's *Exclusion and Embrace: A Theological Exploration of Identity, Otherness,* and *Reconciliation* (Nashville: Abingdon Press, 1996); and George Pavlich's chapter, "What Are Dangers As Well As the Promises of Community Involvement?" in *Critical Issues in Restorative Justice,* eds. Howard Zehr and Barb Toews (Monsey, NY: Criminal Justice Press, 2004).

10 *Beyond the Walls—The Road to Redemption* is written and directed by Teya Sepinuck of TOVA, a theater program that gives voice to the voiceless. See www.tovaartisticprojects.org.

11 The word "story" means different things to different people. It may refer to lies, saying what one thinks another wants to hear, or putting on masks to hide one's true thoughts and feelings. If the word "story" does not resonate with you, find another word to express the idea of speaking from the heart about your experiences.

12 From the Office of the Victim Advocate, Harrisburg, Pennsylvania.

13 For a fuller discussion of victims' experiences, see Zehr, *Transcending.*

14 See Khamisa, *From Murder to Forgiveness*, p.1.

15 See Zehr, *Transcending*, p. 36.

16 Ibid., p. 126.

17 See Khamisa, *From Murder to Forgiveness*, p. 80.
18 See Zehr, *Transcending*, p. 115.
19 Ibid., p. 14.
20 Ibid., p. 34.
21 Ibid., p. 50.
22 From the Pennsylvania Prison Society, Day of Responsibility, in collaboration with Department of Corrections; State Correctional Institution (SCI)—Dallas L.I.F.E. Assocation; and SCI-Retreat Community Development Organization.
23 See Howard Zehr, *Doing Life: Reflections of Men and Women Serving Life Sentences* (Intercourse, PA: Good Books, 1996), p. 73.
24 A prisoner sentiment frequently heard in my work at the Pennsylvania Prison Society.
25 See Zehr, *Doing Life*, p. 88.
26 From *Beyond the Walls—The Road to Redemption.*
27 See Zehr, *Doing Life*, p. 114-115.
28 Ibid., p. 22.
29 A prisoner sentiment frequently heard in my work at the Pennsylvania Prison Society.
30 See Zehr, *Doing Life*, p. 50.
31 Ibid., p. 22.
32 From Transitional Conferencing and Minnesota Department of Corrections. For more on Transitional Conferencing, see www.transitionalconferencing.org and Minnesota Department of Corrections.
33 See *A Sentence of Their Own,* a documentary by Edgar A. Barens, 2001.
34 Ibid.
35 See Ann Adalist-Estrin and Jim Mustin, *Responding to Children and Families of Prisoners: A Community Guide* (Family and Corrections Network, 2003).
36 See *When the Bough Breaks: Children of Mothers in Prison*, a documentary by Filmakers Library, 2001.
37 A prisoners sentiment frequently heard in my work at the Pennsylvania Prison Society.
38 Ibid.
39 See San Francisco Partnership for Incarcerated Parents, Children of Incarcerated Parents: Bill of Rights (2003).
40 Suzette, a wife and mother of incarcerated family members, tells of this experience in *Beyond the Walls—The Road to Redemption*.
41 For more general information about face-to-face meetings, refer to the following associations: Victim-Offender Mediation Association (www.voma.org) and European Forum for Victim-Offender Mediation and Restorative Justice (www.euforumrj.org).
42 See Kay Pranis, Barry Stuart, and Mark Wedge, *Peacemaking Circles: From Crime to Community* (St. Paul, MN: Living Justice Press, 2003), 78-79. For more information about Circles, also see Kay Pranis, *The Little Book of Circle Processes* (Intercourse, PA: Good Books, 2005).

43 See Allan MacRae and Howard Zehr, *The Little Book of Family Group Conferences: New Zealand Style* (Intercourse, PA: Good Books, 2004), 62-64. This book provides a fuller explanation of FGCs.

44 This story is from the Office of the Victim Advocate, Mediation Program for Victims of Violent Crime, Harrisburg, Pennsylvania. For more information about mediation, see *Meeting with a Killer* (Lucky Duck Productions) and *Beyond Conviction* by Tied to the Tracks Film, Inc; and Lorraine Stutzman Amstutz and Howard Zehr, "Victim-Offender Conferencing in Pennsylvania's Juvenile Justice System," available online at www.mcc.org/us/peaceandjustice/crime.html.

45 From Kirk Blackard, *Restoring Peace: Using Lessons from Prison to Mend Broken Relationships* (Victoria, BC: Trafford Publishing, 2004). For more information about group dialogues, refer to the *Restoring Peace Offender Study Guide;* the Sycamore Tree Project, a program of Prison Fellowship International Centre for Justice and Reconciliation; and Citizens, Victims, Offenders Restoring Justice Project, a project of University of Minnesota Center for Restorative Justice and Peacemaking.

46 From Community Justice Initiatives in Waterloo, Ontario, a program that assists women in making the transition from prison to community. For more information, see the Correctional Services Canada website at www.csc-scc.gc.ca; and the video *No One Is Disposable: Circles of Support and Accountability,* available through Mennonite and Brethren in Christ Center, www.mbicresourcecenter.org.

47 For more information, see MacRae and Zehr, *Family Group Conferencing.*

48 Used by permission from the Minnesota Department of Corrections, Circle of Healing, Minnesota Correction Facility, Shakopee, Minn.

49 For information on organizing all the tasks necessary to start a restorative-justice, specifically mediation, program, see Susan Sharpe, *Restorative Justice: A Vision for Healing and Change* (Edmonton, AB: Mediation and Restorative Justice Center, 1998). It's also useful for people in prison.

50 Much material on restorative discipline is currently framed around schools. Yet, it has implications in prison. For more information, see the Lorraine Stutzman Amstutz and Judy Mullet, *The Little Book of Restorative Discipline for Schools* (Intercourse, PA: Good Books, 2005).

51 See Sandra Bloom, *Creating Sanctuary: Toward an Evolution of Sane Societies* (New York: Routledge, 1997) and Judith Herman, *Trauma and Recovery* (New York: BasicBooks, 1997).

52 Used by permission from the Minnesota Department of Corrections.

53 The premise behind "pay it forward" is that you cannot always pay someone back, but you can pay your gratitude or amends forward to someone else who may need your help. See the book *Pay it Forward* by Catherine Ryan Hide (New York: Pocket Books, 2004), or the movie by same name by Warner Bros.

Selected Readings

Blackard, Kirk (2004). *Restoring Peace: Using Lessons from Prison to Mend Broken Relationships.* Victoria, BC: Trafford Publishing.

Breton, Denise and Stephen Lehman (2001). *The Mystic Heart of Justice: Restoring Wholeness in a Broken World.* West Chester, PA: Chrysalis Books.

Casarjian, Robin (1995). *Houses of Healing: A Prisoner's Guide to Inner Power and Freedom.* Boston: The Lionheart Foundation.

Gilligan, James (2001). *Preventing Violence.* New York: Thames and Hudson.

Herman, Judith (1997). *Trauma and Recovery.* New York: BasicBooks.

McCaslin, Wanda, ed. (2005). *Justice as Healing: Indigenous Ways: Writings on Community Peacemaking and Restorative Justice from the Native Law Centre.* St. Paul: Living Justice Press.

Pranis, Kay, Barry Stuart, and Mark Wedge (2003). *Peacemaking Circles: From Crime to Community.* St. Paul: Living Justice Press.

Ross, Rupert (1996). *Returning to the Teachings: Exploring Aboriginal Justice.* New York: Penguin Books.

Zehr, Howard (1990/2005). *Changing Lenses: A New Focus on Crime and Justice*. Scottdale, PA: Herald Press.

Zehr, Howard (1996). *Doing Life: Reflections of Men and Women Serving Life Sentences.* Intercourse, PA: Good Books.

Zehr, Howard (2001). *Transcending: Reflections of Crime Victims.* Intercourse, PA: Good Books.

Please refer to the endnotes for other books, videos, and Web resources. For restorative-justice Web sites and a larger resource list, see www.restorativejustice.org.

The following books in the *The Little Books of Justice and Peacebuilding* series (all published by Good Books) may be helpful:

— ***The Little Book of Restorative Justice***

— ***The Little Book of Family Group Conferences***

— ***The Little Book of Circle Processes***

— ***The Little Book of Restorative Discipline for Schools***

— ***The Little Book of Trauma Healing***

About the Author

Barb Toews is a Program Manager with the Pennsylvania Prison Society, a position in which she creates and facilitates a variety of restorative-justice projects, incorporates the philosophy into offender-oriented programs, and collaborates with incarcerated men and women as they develop their own restorative projects. Prior to this position, she was the founding director of the Lancaster Area Victim-Offender Reconciliation Program in Lancaster, PA. She is an experienced trainer, educator, and practitioner of restorative justice and Victim-Offender Mediation.

She has published a variety of articles about restorative justice and co-edited, with Howard Zehr, the anthology, *Critical Issues in Restorative Justice* (Monsey, NY: Criminal Justice Press, 2004). Barb holds a master's degree in conflict transformation from Eastern Mennonite University in Harrisonburg, VA.

A list of study questions to enrich personal reflection or group discussion of this book is available (free of charge) on the Good Books Web site at www.GoodBooks.com.

METHOD OF PAYMENT

❒ Check or Money Order
(*payable to **Good Books** in U.S. funds*)

❒ Please charge my:
❒ MasterCard ❒ Visa
❒ Discover ❒ American Express

____

exp. date ______________________________

Signature ______________________________

Name ______________________________

Address ______________________________

City ______________________________

State ______________________________

Zip ______________________________

Phone ______________________________

Email ______________________________

SHIP TO: (if different)

Name ______________________________

Address ______________________________

City ______________________________

State ______________________________

Zip ______________________________

If this book is being mailed to a prison, please provide prison requirements for mailing books into that particular facility.

Group Discounts for

The Little Book of Restorative Justice for People in Prison

ORDER FORM

If you would like to order multiple copies of ***The Little Book of Restorative Justice for People in Prison*** by Barb Toews for groups you know or are a part of, use this form. (Discounts apply only for more than one copy.)

Photocopy this page as often as you like.

The following discounts apply:

1 copy	$4.95
2-5 copies	$4.45 each (a 10% discount)
6-10 copies	$4.20 each (a 15% discount)
11-20 copies	$3.96 each (a 20% discount)
21-99 copies	$3.45 each (a 30% discount)
100 or more	$2.97 each (a 40% discount)

Prices subject to change.

FREE shipping on orders of 100 copies or more to continental U.S. For other bulk shipping rates e-mail custserv@GoodBooks.com

Quantity ***Price*** ***Total***

____ copies of ***People in Prison*** @ ______ _______

PA residents add 6% sales tax _______

Shipping & Handling

(U.S. orders only: add 10%; $3.00 minimum) _______

TOTAL _______